T0324188

"The authors address a debated topic i
standable for anyone. The authors do
various sides responding to them and ⎯ ⎯⎯ ...ng their position. They
do this in a way that is encouraging."

—EMMANUEL ENGULU, adjunct professor, Eternity Bible College;
adjunct professor, Denver Seminary;
pastor, Providence Bible Church, Denver

"In *Conquerors Not Captives*, Joseph Dodson and Mattie Motl combine scholarship and wit in a way that brings about new clarity to Romans 7 and gives life to our relationship with God. Simply put, they deliver immanent scholarship with a pastoral heart."

—ROBERT GELINAS, lead pastor, Colorado Community Church

"On the hot topic of the 'I' of Romans 7, Dodson and Motl model expert exegesis: attentive to historical context, insightful reading of Romans as a whole, and inspiring in terms of understanding Pauline theology and biblical theology more widely. Concise, well-written—and convincing!"

—NIJAY K. GUPTA, professor of New Testament, Northern Seminary

"Space lacks for me to express to the reader what a wonderful book this is. With this book you are in the hands of one of today's most accomplished interpreters of Paul, but you are also in the hands of pastors. This combination is rare—the church needs it more than ever. Here is a fantastic start on a chapter of the Bible that is crucial for the spiritual health of the Christian. My hunch is that this will become one of those books that you want to put in the hands of all your friends."

—OSVALDO PADILLA, professor, Beeson Divinity School

"Putting my bias on the table: I am one who has been learning from Joseph R. Dodson (and his daughter Mattie) for many years. Having resonated with his arguments about Romans 7 for some time, I am grateful to see them put into print to help generations of readers gain clarity. What I want to do I *can* do: heartily endorse this book!"

—MADISON N. PIERCE, associate professor of New Testament,
Western Theological Seminary

"The popular view of Romans 7 as describing a 'believer' is difficult to defeat because so many people resonate with it. However, as students of the Scriptures we don't first ask if it fits our experience, but rather inquire as to what the text says. Dodson and Motl's book covers the complicated ground of Romans 7 in a winsome and pastoral way, arguing that Christians are not captives but conquerors. This is the best short summary of Romans 7 that I have read. It includes the history of interpretation, the larger context, and careful exegesis of the passage itself. Those who disagree must reckon with the arguments in this book."

—PATRICK SCHREINER, associate professor of New Testament and biblical theology, Midwestern Baptist Theological Seminary; author of *The Visual Word*, *The Kingdom of God and the Glory of the Cross*, and *The Ascension of Christ*

CONQUERORS NOT CAPTIVES

Reframing Romans 7
for the Christian Life

CONQUERORS NOT CAPTIVES

Reframing Romans 7
for the Christian Life

Joseph R. Dodson
with Mattie Mae Motl

LEXHAM PRESS

Conquerors Not Captives: Reframing Romans 7 for the Christian Life

Copyright 2024 Joseph R. Dodson and Mattie Mae Motl

Lexham Press, 1313 Commercial St., Bellingham, WA 98225
LexhamPress.com

Print ISBN 9781683597704
Digital ISBN 9781683597711
Library of Congress Control Number 2023948050

Lexham Editorial: Derek R. Brown, Katrina Smith, James Spinti,
    Mandi Newell
Cover Design: Lydia Dahl
Typesetting: Abigail Stocker

23 24 25 26 27 28 29 / US / 12 11 10 9 8 7 6 5 4 3 2 1

To Iain Roman Richard Dodson,
our gentle giant,
beloved son and brother,
Midge's manny and Caspian's tutor

Contents

Foreword

I'll never forget meeting Joseph (I'll call him Joey) in the office of Dr. Simon Gathercole at Aberdeen University, Scotland, in the summer of 2004. We were both doing doctoral studies under Simon, and both of us were researching Paul's letter to the Romans. We chitchatted a bit, but it wasn't more than a few minutes before we were talking about Romans 7. I had always thought that the popular reading of Romans 7:14–25—that Paul is describing a Christian's struggle with sin—to be a misinterpretation of what Paul was actually arguing for at that point in the letter. No doubt, I do personally resonate with some of Paul's language there, and so have many Christians throughout the ages. Sometimes I feel like I'm overcome by sin and that my flesh is getting the best of me. From a practical standpoint, I get it. I'm among many Christians who find solace in Paul's words. Maybe I'm not that bad. After all, Paul struggled with sin too!

But Romans 7 doesn't talk about a person struggling with sin. He talks about a person being defeated by and enslaved to sin. When read within the context of Paul's larger argument in Romans 5–8, especially how 7:14–25 relates to the Christian experience described in 8:1–11, Romans 7 can hardly be describing the life of person indwelt by the Holy Spirit.

And Joey agreed. Not only did he agree, but like the proverbial kid in the candy shop, Joey was elated that he not only found a friend—we've been best friends ever since—but someone who was thrilled to have lengthy conversations about the exegetical nuances and literary placement of Paul's pericope in Romans 7:14–25. There aren't too many of us in the world.

While Joey and I agreed on Paul's meaning in Romans 7, he clearly had done more research on the passage than I had. "You should write a book on Romans 7," I told Joey. Over the years, Joey has engaged in many different topics and has written several books. But his passion for understanding Romans 7 has always been lingering in the background. And, finally, after marinating in the chapter for over two decades, Joey has written that book.

Three things particularly stand out to me about Joey's *Conquerors Not Captives*. First, I found the first two chapters on historical interpretations of Romans 7 to be incredibly enlightening. I've been fairly aware of the exegetical arguments for how to understand the chapter, but I wasn't aware of how other church leaders had understood it. Second, I think Joey does a fantastic job situating Romans 7:14–25 in the larger literary context of Romans 5–8. I think many interpreters read Romans 7 the way my kids used to cross the street when they were young—looking neither to the left nor the right. We cannot begin to understand what Paul meant in Romans 7 until we look to the left (Rom 5–6) and to the right (Rom 8). Only then should we proceed with caution. Finally, I most of all appreciate how Joey is able to keep his scholarly wits about him without writing a boring book. Joey writes with both buttery prose and scholarly depth; he weaves in pop culture without being like that typical cringy professor who thinks they're being relevant. This book is a piece of exemplary scholarship that is exegetically responsible, ecclesiologically practical, and it's just down right fun to read.

I can't promise you'll agree with Joey's conclusion or all his arguments. But I feel very confident that you'll enjoy the journey.

Preston Sprinkle, PhD
author, speaker, podcaster

Acknowledgments

Rome wasn't built in a day, and this book on Romans 7 wasn't written that quickly either. Nor was it completed alone. I have so many people to thank that I'm confident I'll accidently leave someone out. My sincere apologies if that is you. I'd like to start by thanking Derek Brown and Mike Bird for asking me to write this book in the first place, as well as all the fine people at Lexham. Next, I appreciate Bart Patton and the great folks at Southern Methodist University and Perkins School of Theology for the Birdwell Library Fellowship that helped me kick off my research for this project. I'd also like to thank my seminary president, Mark Young, and provost, Don Payne, for giving me the Craig L. Blomberg Chair of New Testament, which afforded me monies to write most of this book in Cambridge (in the company of the honorable Craig Blomberg himself no less). On that note, thanks also to Peter Williams and Tyndale House for hosting me while I was there.

I particularly appreciate Madison Pierce and Will Timmins for reading a draft of this book and providing me with super helpful pushbacks. Thanks also to my friends and Denver Seminary students who made comments and who served as conversation partners during the process, especially Kinnon Dodson, Loren Dowdy, Rick Eisenberg, Emmanuel Engulu, Kendal Land, Arisson Stanfield, Tully Borland, Ryan Tafilowski,

Nick Quinn, and Brandon Young. I, of course, appreciate my best friend for writing the foreword and for having me promote the book on his podcast. I surely can't forget Hannah Harris, Josh DeLeon and Samuel Woo, who worked tirelessly as my research assistants, chasing down countless footnotes and random resources.

Thanks also to my wife for her never-ending support for what she thought was a never-ending project. Finally, what an indescribable privilege it was to write this book with my daughter. She did so while having and raising Midge (the best granddaughter in the multiverse!), taking full loads of seminary classes, and working with teens for a crisis pregnancy ministry. I stand amazed. Of course, this project would have been nearly impossible without the help of my son and Midge's "manny": Iain Roman Richard Dodson. Therefore, it is to him that we dedicate this book.

Preface

This book seeks to offer those in the classroom and the church an explanation of a nearly established interpretation in the academy regarding the identity of the wretch in Romans 7:14–25. That is, many scholars (if not most) reject the popular position that Paul speaks here from his own perspective as a believer unable to overcome his fleshly desires. These scholars also do not consider the passage as intending to represent the captivity Christ-followers will experience for the rest of their lives. As we will show in the subsequent chapters, this reading contradicts not only Paul's confident assertions in his other letters regarding how the Holy Spirit enables believers to overcome sin, but it also clashes against what he writes in the verses leading up to 7:14–25 and the passages following it.

Most of the early church fathers also did not interpret this monologue as Paul referring to himself in these verses as the miserable creature. And the theologians who first began to endorse that view did so *not* so much from a desire to understand the passage in its original context but more so with an apologetic agenda to correct those who had swung the pendulum too far toward perfectionism. Even then, some of these most influential theologians nuanced their interpretations in pivotal ways often neglected among clergy and laypeople today.

Make no mistake, though, this is not a useless, ivory tower affair. It is a meaningful concern with real world implications. How we understand the tormented figure of Romans 7 determines how we read the promises in Romans 8 and the rest of the New Testament. For example, if the passage refers to Paul as a helpless believer and to the gloomy expectations for the Christian life, we may be persuaded to interpret the New Testament assurances about liberation from sin differently—hyperbolic or maybe even hollow.

Although we will present possible identities for the *I* in Romans 7 and highlight the view we endorse, we will mostly endeavor to discount the blunt and clumsy popular view that leads believers to think they, too, are impotent before sin and powerless to do good. Of course, we realize we are attempting a Herculean task here, if not a fool's errand. Since many people are so deeply rooted in this familiar position, any other reading seems absurd. We hope to encourage readers such as this to at least move Romans 7 to the edge of the desk rather than keeping it in the center when it comes to understanding sanctification, moral progression, and our relationship with the flesh. At the core of these discussions should instead be the verses asserting how even though sin still harasses the Christ-follower, it does not reign over her. In other words, believers should give priority to those passages that promise God's deliverance from both the penalty and power of sin and to those scriptures proclaiming how Christ and his indwelling Spirit are more than enough to empower believers to do the things they want to do.

Abbreviations

ACCSNT	Ancient Christian Commentary on Scripture: New Testament
BECNT	Baker Exegetical Commentary on the New Testament
Bib	*Biblica*
BibInt	*Biblical Interpretation*
BibInt	Biblical Interpretation Series
BZNW	Beihefte zur Zeitschrift für die neutestamentliche Wissenschaft
c.	circa
CBET	Contributions to Biblical Exegesis and Theology
CBQ	*Catholic Biblical Quarterly*
ch(s).	chapter(s)
Comm. Rom.	Origen, *Commentarii in Romanos/ Commentary on Romans*
CSB	Christian Standard Bible
CWE	Collected Works of Erasmus
Disc.	Epictetus, *Discourses*
Ep.	Seneca, *Epistulae morales/Moral Epistles*
Epist.	Jerome, *Epistulae/Epistles*
EQ	*Evangelical Quarterly*
esp.	especially

HTR	*Harvard Theological Review*
Inst.	Quintilian, *Institutio Oratio*
JBL	*Journal of Biblical Literature*
JSNT	*Journal for the Study of the New Testament*
JSNTSup	Journal for the Study of the New Testament Supplement
JSPL	*Journal for the Study of Paul and His Letters*
LAE	Life of Adam and Eve
LCL	Loeb Classical Library
Leg.	Philo, *Legum Allegoriae/Allegorical Interpretation*
LNTS	Library of New Testament Studies
LW	*Luther's Works: The American Edition.* 55 vols. St. Louis: Concordia, 1955–1986.
Metam.	Ovid, *Metamorphoses*
MNTC	Moffatt New Testament Commentary
NCB	New Century Bible
Neot	*Neotestamentica*
NIB	Keck, Leander E., ed. *New Interpreter's Bible.* 12 vols. Nashville: Abingdon, 1994–2004.
NICNT	New International Commentary on the New Testament
NIGTC	New International Greek Testament Commentary
NLT	New Living Translation
NovT	*Novum Testamentum*
NovTSup	Novum Testamentum Supplements
NPNF	Schaff, Philip, and Henry Wace, eds. *A Select Library of Nicene and Post-Nicene Fathers of the Christian Church.* 28 vols. in 2 series. 1886–1889.
NTS	*New Testament Studies*

Opif.	Philo, *De opificio mundi/On the Creation of the World*
PNTC	Pillar New Testament Commentary
Resp.	Plato, *Respublica/Republic*
RHR	*Revue de l'histoire des religions*
SBLDS	Society of Biblical Literature Dissertation Series
TNTC	Tyndale New Testament Commentaries
TZ	*Theologische Zeitschrift*
Vit. beat.	Seneca, *De vita beata/On the Happy Life*
WA	Hermann, Rudolf, et al., eds. *Luthers Werke.* 127 vols. Weimar: Böhlaus, 1883–2009.
WW	Jackson, Thomas, ed. *The Works of John Wesley.* 3rd ed. 14 vols. London: Wesleyan Methodist Book Room, 1872.
WUNT	Wissenschaftliche Untersuchungen zum Neuen Testament
ZECNT	Zondervan Exegetical Commentary Series on the New Testament
ZNTW	*Zeitschrift für die neutestamentliche Wissenschaft*

Introduction

It Is No Longer I

According to legend, after his conversion Saint Augustine once passed by a former mistress on the street. Seeing him, she became aroused and yelled: "Augustine, it is I, it is I!" Without missing a beat, though, Augustine turned to her and replied: "Aye, madam: but it is no longer I!"[1] Similarly, in his letters, the apostle Paul makes it clear that anyone in Christ is a new creation—the old is gone, the new has come. This means, like Augustine, the believer too can finally turn to temptation and say, "Aye, but it is no longer I." When it comes to the church's relationship with temptation, the apostle spells it out over and again: sin is no longer the boss. Consequently, evil desires, anger, and lust should not govern, rule, or dominate those who serve the Lord.

---

1. C. H. Spurgeon, "The Way to Honor," in vol. 19 of *Metropolitan Tabernacle Pulpit: Sermons Preached and Revised by C. H. Spurgeon during the Year 1873* (London: Passmore & Alabaster, 1874), sermon no. 1118.

In Galatians, for instance, Paul commands believers to live by the power of the Spirit so that they will not indulge their worldly desires. Sure, he admits, the flesh opposes the Spirit and the Spirit opposes the flesh; but this, he concludes, is why believers must no longer choose to do the shameful things they want to do. Since it was for freedom that Christ has set his people free, they should not use this newfound liberty to satisfy their lusts. The fruit of the Spirit is self-control, and those who belong to the Lord have crucified the flesh along with its passions and desires. They, like the apostle, have been crucified with Christ and to the world. Now, they no longer live; not they, but Christ lives within them. As a result, they walk stregthened by faith not shackled to sin.

Along with the Galatians, Paul teaches the Thessalonians how holiness is God's will for their lives too. He explains that they should not give in to their lusts like those who treat their bodies as an amusement park rather than as a temple. The apostle concludes the letter praying God himself would sanctify the believers wholly and completely, through and through, so that their body, soul, and spirit would be kept blameless unto the day of the Lord. In case anyone thinks this is a saccharine sentiment, unrealistic hope, or rhetorical pipe dream, Paul punctuates the prayer with a confident assertion: "the one who calls you is faithful, and he will do it" (1 Thess 5:23–24).[2]

The apostle's expectations for believers in Galatians and 1 Thessalonians also line up with what he later tells Titus. God's grace came to teach believers how to say "no" to sin and "yes" to self-control, so that his people would conduct themselves in an upright and godly manner while they wait for the coming of the Lord—"who gave himself for us to redeem us from all

---

2. Unless otherwise noted, all translations are from the NIV.

wickedness and to purify for himself a people that are his very own" (Titus 2:14). Of course, as Paul warns elsewhere, believers can certainly still fall and will constantly face temptation, but when they do God will be faithful to "provide the way out" (1 Cor 10:13).

The theme of righteous living also recurs in Romans. There, the apostle tells the believers they should no longer live like sin is their master. Since we died with Christ to sin, how then, Paul asks, can we live in it any longer? The Lord was not crucified just so his people could be forgiven, but he was also raised that they could be free—counting themselves dead to sin but alive to God in Christ Jesus. Therefore, believers are to be the Lord's obedient servants: no longer slaves to sin but children of righteousness, reaping the benefit of holiness, resulting in lasting life. This good news rings forth: the church no longer has any obligation to obey the tyranny of sin. Instead, by the Spirit they can now put to death the misdeeds of their bodies so that they will live. For this reason, by God's grace and in his love, those who have been redeemed are to lay aside the deeds of darkness and put on the armor of light, clothing themselves with Christ and giving no quarter or provision to the flesh and its paltry desires.

These passages dovetail together to underline a decisive gospel truth. Because of what the Lord has done, his followers must no longer live in bondage to sin. Instead, they should now walk in holiness, righteousness, and self-control. The common thread of these passages reminds us of a quotation from Martin Luther, which goes something like this: "Before I understood the truth of the gospel, whenever sin would knock on my door, I would answer it. But now that I know Christ lives within me, whenever sin knocks, I let him get the door."[3] To play off this illustration, the promise in Paul's letters is that though sin will continue to stand at the door and knock, believers no longer have to open it. Instead, they can ask the Lord to answer it for them. Then, as Luther goes on to state, at the sight of the nail-pierced hands and punctured side, sin will promptly retreat.

Despite these verses and their promises, one passage is the outlier that dampens the mood and rains on the parade. It is Romans 7:14–25, which at first glance seems to fly in the face of everything the apostle had written and would go on to write.

> I am unspiritual, sold as a slave to sin. I do not understand what I do. For what I want to do I do not do, but what I hate I do. And if I do what I do not want to do, I agree that the law is good. As it is, it is no longer I myself who do it, but it is sin living in me. For I know that good itself does not dwell in me, that is, in my sinful nature. For I have the desire to do what is good, but I cannot carry it out. For I do not do the good I want to do, but the evil I do not want to do—this I keep on doing. Now if I do what I do not want to do, it is no longer I who do it, but it is sin living in me that does it.
>
> So I find this law at work: Although I want to do good, evil is right there with me. For in my inner being I delight in God's law; but I see another law at work in me, waging war against the law of my mind and making me a prisoner of the law of sin at work within me. What a wretched man I am! Who will rescue me from this body that is subject to death? Thanks be to God, who delivers me through Jesus Christ our Lord!

---

3. Although this may be apocryphal, see R. Kent Hughes, *Luke: That You May Know the Truth*, Preaching the Word (Wheaton, IL: Crossway, 2015), 140.

> So then, I myself in my mind am a slave to God's law,
> but in my sinful nature a slave to the law of sin.

Emma Wasserman points out how this passage has been placed at the center of the Christian understanding of sin more than any other selection of Scripture. This is ironic, she notes, since Romans 7 is the anomaly compared to what the rest of the New Testament says about how the Spirit permits and compels a believer to overcome the flesh.[4]

What's more, confusion over the exact identity of the I abounds. Is Paul talking about himself or someone else? Is the I, to borrow from Jan Lambrecht, "radically fictitious" or "thoroughly autobiographical" or "to a certain extent both at the same time?" In other words, is the passage meant to describe the predicament of a Christian, a nonbeliever, or both? More pointedly, is Paul's portrayal here altogether unrelated to those whom Christ has liberated, or is it to say that as long as Christians live on this earth, they will be wretched?[5] All these questions evoke the line by e. e. cummings: "who are you, little i."

Because of this confusion, as Susan Eastman states, few passages in the apostle's letters have caused "more consternation and received more attention" than this one.[6] Nevertheless, many (if not most) Pauline scholars reject the interpretation that these verses in 7:14–25 depict the apostle's life as a Christian. A growing chorus also dismisses the notion that Paul intends the wretch's monologue in this passage to describe a believer's relationship with sin, which, as will be shown below, was not the view of the first interpreters of Romans either.

---

4. Emma Wasserman, "The Death of the Soul in Romans 7: Revisiting Paul's Anthropology in Light of Hellenistic Moral Psychology," *JBL* 126 (2007): 793.

5. Jan Lambrecht, *The Wretched "I" and Its Liberation* (Grand Rapids: Eerdmans, 1992), 72.

6. Susan Eastman, *Paul and the Person* (Grand Rapids: Eerdmans, 2017), 109.

Yet against the grain of many early Church theologians and modern scholars, countless pastors and believers today confidently subscribe to the explanation that Paul portrays the normal Christian experience in Romans 7. Because of this, 7:14–25 is a consequential passage for how the church understands Paul's view of life inside of Christ.[7] As James Dunn concludes, our position here "will in large measure determine our understanding of Paul's theology as a whole."[8] For instance, if one takes the view that Romans 7 describes the typical believer's life as powerless before sin, then, to borrow from Ernst Käsemann, everything that Paul says about items such as baptism and justification will need to be interpreted differently—as overstated, paradoxical, or extreme.[9] In addition to theology, one's interpretation here also has bearings on anthropology, psychology, and pastoral counseling.

As we will see in chapter 2, even those who first began to promote the position that the I refers to Paul did so to confront the drastic notion that a person can be perfect and without sin. Yet, the "never sin again" ledge is not the precipice most modern Christians are in danger of falling from. Rather, it is down the slippery slope on the other side that many tend to slide, resigning to be slaves to sin and unable do the good they desire. On that side of the ledge, the total impotence in Romans 7, it is assumed, represents the common Christian experience.

Not only does this much-touted view collide with what Scripture says elsewhere, it usually leads believers to think moral failure is inevitable. (If a person wakes up each day

---

7. Ben Witherington III, *Paul's Letter to the Romans: A Socio-Rhetorical Commentary* (Grand Rapids: Eerdmans, 2004), 193.

8. James Dunn, "Romans 7.14–25 in the Theology of Paul," *TZ* 31 (1975): 257.

9. Ernst Käsemann, *Commentary on Romans*, trans. G. W. Bromiley (Grand Rapids: Eerdmans, 1980), 211.

convinced sin is going to win, hasn't it won already?) In other words, this popular interpretation of Romans 7 often reinforces a despair at being defeated by unwanted desires. With that view, we can do all things through Christ, except, it seems, live a godly life. Or, along those lines, from this perspective, God can do immeasurably more than we can ask for or imagine, aside from enabling us to overcome our flesh. As Mark Reasoner argues, with this interpretation, "the healing and sanctifying power of grace" is often minimized, and ongoing sinfulness more openly accepted.[10] As a result, to borrow from Hae-Kyung Chang, Christ-followers take comfort in believing that Paul is their partner in inevitable sin and therefore resign themselves to defeat.[11]

We too have regularly heard this popular reading used to excuse personal sin. A severe example is when I asked one of my former parishioners how he could abandon his wife and daughters for another woman, to which he shrugged and said, "Like Paul, the things I want to do, I do not do." In our minds, more than of Paul, this flippant surrender to sin sounds like the Emily Dickinson line: "the heart wants what it wants, or else it does not care." But we are persuaded that the apostle did not mean for Romans 7 to represent the normal Christian life—his own or otherwise. For us, the attempt to simultaneously maintain that believers are both set free from sin while also enslaved to sin represents a contradiction rather than a tension. In contrast to a resignation of powerlessness, which the popular interpretation of Romans 7 can lead to, the proper reading of the passage displays a fresh, more poignant truth.

---

10. Mark Reasoner, *Romans in Full Circle: A History of Interpretation* (Louisville: Westminster John Knox, 2005), 76.

11. Hae-Kyung Chang, "The Christian Life in a Dialectical Tension? Rom 7:7–25," *NovT* 49 (2007): 258.

That is, unlike the I in Romans 7, we no longer have to answer sin's call and solicitation.

Our thesis is this: looking at Romans 7 in context rules out the view that Paul meant to present here the typical Christian life and the plight of a mature believer. Instead, those dedicated to the Lord increasingly experience freedom from sin because of the Spirit's empowerment for them to put to death the misdeeds of their body.[12] Rather than ongoing subjugation to sin, God's people should expect to experience a liberated life in Christ.[13] When rightly interpreted, then, Romans 7 plays a part in demonstrating that by the grace of God, through the example of his Son, in the power of his Spirit, and with the help of his church, holiness is not only a possibility: it is an ever-pressing, hope-filled responsibility.

While some readers may be encouraged by the suggestion that Christ-followers can indeed lead a triumphant life over sin (even as they still struggle with temptations and desires), others may initially feel threatened by this claim and consider the notion unrealistic, if not legalistic. Therein lies a key aim of this book. In the following pages, we will attempt to humbly revisit Romans 7 as part of Paul's gospel intended to promote a biblical, prudent, and practical view of increasing victory over sin that is full of mercy, kindness, grace, and joy. Our reading of Romans 7 does not result in any judgmental finger-wagging and disapproving browbeating, but to authentic freedom and love. It also coheres with the overarching purpose of Romans:

---

12. Michael J. Gorman, *Romans: A Theological and Pastoral Commentary* (Grand Rapids: Eerdmans, 2022), 184.

13. Craig S. Keener, *The Mind of the Spirit: Paul's Approach to Transformed Thinking* (Grand Rapids: Baker Academic, 2016), 63.

to call the church "to the obedience that comes from faith for his name's sake" (Rom 1:5).[14]

In our attempt to explain how Romans 7 does not depict a Christian defeated by sin, we will first provide in chapters 1–2 a survey of two broad views regarding whether Paul refers to himself or someone else in 7:14–25. To observe this passage in its original context, chapter 3 goes back to Romans 5 and follows the line of reasoning on to Romans 8—where Paul does discuss how Christians should live in relation to sin and their fleshly desires. Once we have done this, in chapter 4, we will walk through a brief exposition of 7:14–25. The next chapter then makes a case against the popular view by looking at what the apostle says about himself and about the believer's relationship with sin elsewhere. Chapters 6–7 answer the major rebuttals from those holding to the common position. Next, chapter 8 provides options for whom the I is meant to be. In the conclusion, we will summarize reasons why Paul chose to use the I in the first place. Finally, we discuss the pastoral significance and personal relevance a proper understanding of Romans 7 yields for the Christian life.

Three short notes before proceeding on. First, there is no great way to refer to the I in Romans 7. Scholars do so differently: (1) as we just did, the I; (2) the *ego*, which is the Greek word for "I"; (3) the *I*-figure; and (4) the wretch, captive, or miserable creature, which draws on the self-designation in 7:25. While none of these options are perfect, all of them are viable. Therefore, we will use each of them interchangeably.

Next, unless otherwise specified, when we use the term "law" throughout the book, it refers to the Mosaic law, also

---

14. See Jason A. Myers, *Paul, The Apostle of Obedience: Reading Obedience in Romans*, LNTS 668 (London: T&T Clark, 2022).

called the Torah. This is most often Paul's meaning when he uses the Greek term *nomos*, which is important to keep in mind, lest one neglect the particular intramural and cultural nature of Romans 7.

Third and most importantly, we admit believers' hearts are still prone to wander and inclined to fall. We all tend to be complicitous in sin even as we are molested by it. What's more, on our own, we discover and invent evil, ratify and extend it.[15] Nevertheless, there is a monumental difference between the enslaved wretch in Romans 7 and a liberated believer in the Lord Jesus Christ: namely, in the face of her Adamic condition, the latter has the Spirit who enables her to grow in godliness and who energizes her to deny sin more and more. As Michael Gorman puts it, "Believers still must struggle not to allow Sin to regain mastery, but they do so on the assumption of their liberation from Sin, not their slavery to it."[16]

---

15. Cf. Cornelius Plantinga, *Not the Way It's Supposed to Be: A Breviary of Sin* (Grand Rapids: Eerdmans, 1996). No matter how much we grow in holiness, God's grace will remain "permanently at odds" with our natural, post-Adamic condition. John M. G. Barclay, *Paul and the Gift* (Grand Rapids: Eerdmans, 2015), 503.

16. Gorman, *Romans*, 183. Cf. Don J. Payne, *Already Sanctified: A Theology of the Christian Life in Light of God's Completed Work* (Grand Rapids: Baker Academic, 2020), 10–11.

1 ∿

Not Paul at All

The Wretch Is Someone Else

The next two chapters provide a simple survey of the different readings of Romans 7. Those familiar with the discourse surrounding the *I*-figure will rightly laugh at our use of the word *simple*, since the identity of the wretch is a riddle, wrapped in a mystery, buried in an enigma. Michael Bird even introduces this passage in his commentary by likening it to the incoming turbulence a pilot warns passengers about, so as to say, "fasten your exegetical seatbelts, because this is where it gets bumpy!"[1]

Our first attempt to navigate the interpretive traditions surrounding Romans 7 will fall under the two subheadings: Not Paul and Totally Paul. This chapter will focus on the former view, which argues the apostle is talking about *someone else* in Romans 7:14–25. In the next chapter, we will look at the Totally

---

1. Michael Bird, *Romans*, Story of God Bible Commentary (Grand Rapids, Zondervan, 2016), 230.

Paul reading, which concludes the apostle is indeed referring to *himself as a believer* in the passage. While we admit this is an oversimplification, what generally separates these two groups regards (1) those who think the moral failings of the wretch indicate that Paul writes from the perspective of an unbeliever, and (2) those who think the apostle's mention of desiring to do good and of delighting in the law proves he is talking about himself.[2]

We are not yet aiming to argue for one of these interpretations over the other. We are merely providing a general lay of the land. Therefore, this survey is not meant to be exhaustive but focuses instead on some of the earliest players, since, to quote Faulkner, "The past is never dead. It's not even past." That is to say, as we will see in the following chapters, many of today's views unpack, expand, nuance, or tweak these earlier perspectives.

Regarding the Not Paul view, there is a long history of interpreters who considered the apostle to be referring to somebody else in Romans 7. According to Gerald Bray, "Most of the Fathers believed that here Paul was adopting the persona of an unregenerate man, not describing his own struggles as a Christian." Bray continues, "As far as they were concerned, becoming a Christian would deliver a person from the kind of dilemma the apostle is outlining here."[3] In an attempt to keep this survey simple, we have selected four of the biggest names associated with this reading who significantly demonstrate the

---

2. See Mark A. Seifrid, "Romans 7: The Voice of the Law, the Cry of Lament, and the Shout of Thanksgiving," in *Perspectives on Our Struggle with Sin: Three Views of Romans 7*, ed. Terry L. Wilder (Nashville: B&H Academic, 2011), 111–76.

3. Gerald Bray, *Romans*, ACCSNT 6 (Downers Grove, IL: InterVarsity Press, 1998), 189–90. See also Erasmus, *Annotations on Romans*, trans. John B. Payne, CWE 56 (Toronto: University of Toronto Press, 1994), 599B–600B.

overall argument of this view: Origen, Jerome, Erasmus, and John Wesley.

1.1. ORIGEN: THE MASKED MAN

Of the bygone theologians, Origen (c. 185–253) is the first figure who discussed the identity of the wretch. In his *Commentary on the Epistle to the Romans,* he concludes Paul must have used the I-figure to impersonate someone else because the monologue in Romans 7 clashes with what the apostle writes everywhere else. According to Origen, in this passage Paul was following Scripture's customary practice of saints taking on "the personae of sinners," and of a writer putting on a mask and speaking as that person, like an actor in a play (*Comm Rom.* 6:37).

For Origen, Paul presents the agony of "those who are in the flesh and sold into slavery under sin." The wretch behind the mask represents the man in whom Christ is "not yet dwelling, nor whose body is a temple of God." Origen argues that Paul, as a good teacher, parrots conventional comments typical for a person "under the pretense of an excuse or accusation." He expounds that the apostle continues the masquerade by underlining the *ego*'s frustration so that, in the desperate voice of the sinner, the apostle, "still wearing the mask of the one whom he has described," exclaims: "'Wretched man that I am! Who will set me free from the body of this death?'" (*Comm. Rom.* 6:37).

According to Origen, Paul briefly breaks character in 7:25a to answer the miserable creature's desperate cry. Because the apostle cannot bear the suspense, Origen explains, Paul feels compelled to take off the sinner's mask for a moment to respond to the pitiful lament. The apostle therefore bursts out from behind the wretch's persona and with his true voice proclaims: "Thanks be to God through Jesus Christ our Lord!" (7:25a NASB). Origen argues that Paul then readorns his disguise for the finale.

The mask back in place, the apostle mimics the sinner with this concluding statement: "So then, I myself in my mind am a slave to God's law, but in my sinful nature a slave to the law of sin" (7:25b). Origen goes on to warn how the wrong interpretation of this passage, which presumes the power of sin is so great that even an apostle cannot escape it, yields to "inflicting every soul with despair." This is because, Origen reasons, if Paul cannot overcome his passions, no one can (*Comm. Rom.* 6:42).

Origen anticipates objections to his reading. For anyone asking why Paul would do an impersonation, he explains that, on the one hand, the apostle is faithfully following a biblical pattern where Hebrew saints like David and Daniel did the same. On the other hand, he concludes that by using the disguise, Paul is being sensitive to his audience because the masked man may also refer to weak Christians in the church. The apostle has described these things as if they are going on within himself, lest any of the sinners in the audience be ashamed. Paul does not want these feeble believers to lose heart at the knowledge of their own sins, from which Christ had come to set them free. According to Origen, Paul also adopts this persona to teach a valuable pastoral lesson: since the attraction to sin is fierce, the mortification of the flesh is a gradual process, "not something that happens overnight" (*Comm. Rom.* 6:42–44).

1.2. JEROME: THE PENITENT MAN WILL PASS

Jerome (c. 342–420) translated the Bible into Latin so that ordinary people in his time could read it. In this pursuit to make Scripture accessible to others, he also corresponded with several women to answer their theological questions. In *Epistle* 121, he writes to a prominent lady named Algasia, where he admits how complicated Romans 7 can be to understand. "This entire passage" he tells her, "is wrapped up in excessive obscurity and, if I want to explain it all, I will have to write not just one book, but many long ones" (*Epist.* 121.8). One thing is clear enough to Jerome, however, that he did not need many books to explain. Paul cannot be talking about himself as the wretch, since the apostle was a "vessel of election, whose body was a temple." Jerome reminds Algasia that in Paul, the Holy Spirit dwelled and, through him, Christ spoke. What's more, the apostle himself proclaimed he no longer lived, but that Christ lived within him. So, Jerome spells it out for his friend: Paul "is not speaking about himself, but about the man who, after sinning, wishes to be penitent" (*Epist.* 121.8).

Jerome continues to clarify that, through the miserable creature, Paul describes "the fragility of the human condition, which consists of two men: the inner and the outer, enduring the wars of those fighting amongst themselves." According to Jerome, at the height of despair, this man cries out realizing that all unbelievers are "entangled in the snares of the devil." Like Origen, Jerome infers that Paul takes a break from the impersonation in 7:25 to give thanks to God because, in contrast to the wretch, the apostle was "redeemed through the blood and cast off his dirt in baptism and took up the new clothing of Christ and, from a dead old man, a new man was born." According to Jerome, this provides hope of the same redemption for any who cry "I am a wretched man, who will free me from this body of death?" (*Epist.* 121.8).

Jerome, too, explains that Paul's impersonation here follows the tenor of other biblical heroes who also put on the mask of sinners.

> But if it seems to someone that the apostle does not,
> in his own person, speak about others, let him explain

how Daniel, whom we know to have been just, seems
to be speaking about himself when he prays for others:
"We have sinned, we have acted unjustly, we have carried on unjustly, we have acted impiously and we have
retreated and turned away from your commandments
and judgments and we have not obeyed your servants,
the prophets, who spoke in your name." (*Epist.* 121.8)

1.3. ERASMUS: THE GROSS MAN

Erasmus (c. 1466–1536) published the first Greek New
Testament, which Martin Luther and William Tyndale relied on
for their respective translations. Along with Origen and Jerome,
Erasmus also reckons that Romans 7 portrays a person "subject to so many passions, so many vices, and so many struggles."
In Erasmus's paraphrase, he even has Paul add a parenthetical
statement to signal to the reader that the apostle is imitating
someone else. "As of now, to make my point, I [Paul] have put
on the mask of a man still subject to vices and passions."[4] For
Erasmus, in 7:14–25, Paul's mask represents a carnal Jewish
person under the Mosaic law.[5]

For this enslaved *ego*, Erasmus writes, we should imagine
two men in one: a carnal, "gross man" and a "more pure, less
gross man." He goes on to argue that Paul uses the divided
wretch as a foil for the redeemed, those whom the Lord delivered from the great evils ruling over the carnal person depicted
in the passage. According to Erasmus, the apostle admits that

---

4. See Erasmus, *Opera Omnia* VII 799–801 (LB); and his *Paraphrases on Romans
and Galatians*, ed. Robert D. Sider et al., CWE 42 (Toronto: University of Toronto
Press, 1984).

5. For more on this, see Reasoner, *Romans*, 77.

had he himself not been ransomed, he too would be torn apart in the same way as the captive in Romans 7.[6]

Erasmus declares, over against that I-figure, "We [as believers] have ceased to live by the will of carnal desires and passions" because the law of Christ has liberated us from the law of sin and death. Nevertheless, he reasons, remnants of that former servitude displayed in Romans 7 may remain in some Christians. He asserts, however, that since these believers are now incorporated in Christ, whose law is greater than the power of sin, even those relating to the Romans 7 man "will overcome these and will not be dragged against their will into any serious sin."[7]

1.4. JOHN WESLEY: A TETHERED DOG

John Wesley (1703–1791) also considers Paul to be assuming the role of someone else. In sermon 9, he argues the wretch depicts a man "convinced of sin but not yet delivered from it."[8] Wesley, too, concludes that the apostle "changes the person" and speaks as though he himself is a miserable man under the law. Paul does so, Wesley elaborates, to show in the "most lively manner" the weakness and inefficacy of the law.[9]

Wesley delineates that the character Paul imitates is a person first ignorant of the law, who then comes under the law, which causes him to "sincerely but ineffectually" strive to serve the Lord. But, Wesley writes, the more the miserable creature strives and struggles to be free from sin, the more aware he is of its weight: "the more does he feel his chains, the grievous

---

6. Erasmus, *Paraphrases*, 44.

7. Erasmus, *Paraphrases*, 45.

8. John Wesley, "The Spirit of Bondage and Adoption," *WW* 5:98–111.

9. See Stephen Chester, "The Retrospective View of Romans 7: Paul's Past in Present Perspective" in Wilder, *Perspectives on Our Struggle*, 59–66.

chains of sin, wherewith Satan binds and 'leads him captive at
his will.'" According to Wesley, the *I* is Satan's servant whether
he likes it or not—"though he repine ever so much; though he
rebel, he cannot prevail." Still in bondage to fear and sin, the
man frets and toils without end, "repenting and sinning, and
repenting and sinning again." Like a tethered dog, he may bay,
he may bark, he may bite, but he cannot break his chain. In
this fateful state, "the poor, sinful, helpless wretch" struggles
until he reaches his wit's end when he can barely groan, "'O
wretched man that I am! who shall deliver me from the body
of this death?'"

Considering the context of the entire chapter, Wesley identifies the captive as either a Jewish person or "one under the
Jewish dispensation" who has suffered "heavy, grievous bondage" ever since the law opened his eyes to "the painful light
of hell." To stress how this passage is not meant to describe
Paul or another believer, he expounds that the apostle must be
masked; if not, Scripture contradicts itself. Wesley clarifies: for
the apostle "to have spoken this of himself, or any true believer,
would have been foreign to the whole scope of his discourse;
nay utterly contrary thereto." According to Wesley, the interpretation that Paul is talking about himself especially contravenes what is expressly asserted in Romans 8:2: "because the
law of the Spirit of life in Christ Jesus has set you free from the
law of sin and death." Finally, Wesley reasons, even though sin
remains with a believer it does not *reign* in her. And, while sin
still lingers in the Christian, it is sin, not the Christian, who is
shackled and subdued.

1.5. CONCLUSION

According to the Not Paul view, represented by Origen, Jerome,
Erasmus, and Wesley, the apostle is talking about someone else.

As mentioned in the introduction, like these theologians, many modern scholars consider the context surrounding Romans 7 and Paul's proclamations about believers' power over sin elsewhere as clinching the argument that the apostle is not talking about himself as a Christian in the passage.[10] For these proponents, to believe otherwise not only opposes the apostle's other pronouncements, but can also lead to the absurd conclusion that Christ cannot overcome sin in the believer. With redemption like this, who needs bondage? According to the Not Paul contingent, although the presence of sin remains, the Lord has effectively delivered the believer from its tyranny.

In case you need a refresher at any point in the following pages, here is a chart highlighting four major reasons the Not Paul group thinks the apostle is referring to an unbeliever. We will also elaborate on these throughout the book.

---

1. The immediate context is about how sin manipulates the Mosaic law to produce death.

2. The wretch claims to be a slave to sin, but Paul says believers are no longer slaves to sin.

3. The wretch only mentions sin dwelling within him and never the Holy Spirit.

4. It is ludicrous to assume Christ cannot help the apostle overcome sin.

---

10. As we will see in ch. 8, scholars have posited different explanations of who this miserable creature is.

2 ∿

Totally Paul

The Wretch Is Paul as a Christian

I once was debating the identity of the *ego* with some under-grads, when one of my favorite students interrupted us. She had been eavesdropping on the conversation and could not stay silent any longer. With an endearing Texas accent, she blurted: "It's totally Paul, y'all!" Although not with a Southern drawl, Augustine, Luther, and Calvin share the same sentiment. For them, without a doubt, the wretch behind the mask is Paul. Once again, for the sake of simplicity and brevity, we will limit ourselves to summarizing these three theologians due to their unmistakable influence on this perspective.

Whereas those advocating for the Not Paul position found it inconceivable that this passage refers to the apostle's Christian life, the theologians in this chapter cannot imagine the *I* being anyone other than him because the figure delights in the law of God and desires to do good. We now turn to these heavy hitters who insist the wretch represents the experience of Paul seemingly foiled by the flesh and shackled to sin. As we will see and expand upon more below, these interpreters primarily wield their readings of Romans 7 in a rhetorical campaign against their respective opponents who believe that a person in Christ can be perfect—fully free of the power of sin.

2.1. AUGUSTINE: FREE FROM
SIN BUT NOT ITS DESIRE

Early in his life, Augustine (c. 354–430) initially sided with the Not Paul interpreters. At that time, he concluded 7:14–25 chronicles an unregenerate Jewish person's existence under the law.[1] Back then, Augustine also believed Paul had put himself in the place of this unredeemed man and spoke in that sinner's voice: as someone walking *not* in God's grace but under God's law, frustrated and defeated by the flesh. But, because of debates with opponents who had underemphasized human depravity, Augustine changed his position and concluded that the apostle was talking about himself.[2] As far as we know, this makes Augustine the first theologian who concluded "It's totally Paul, y'all."[3] Reasoner remarks that "it must be emphasized that Augustine's change from interpreting Romans 7 as a pre-Christian experience to a Christian experience was not occasioned by academic 'objective' exegesis"; rather, as Augustine himself admits, he overturned his previous position in response to the "Pelagian threat."[4]

---

1. Reasoner, *Romans*, 70. See Christopher T. Bounds, "Augustine's Interpretation of Romans 7:14–25," in *The Continuing Relevance of Wesleyan Theology: Essays in Honor of Laurence W. Wood*, ed. Nathan Crawford (Eugene, OR: Pickwick, 2011), 15–27.

2. Aquinas argues Rom 7 can be in both ways that Augustine interprets it and considers both interpretations as viable options but prefers Augustine's second take on the passage (Aquinas, *Summa* 7.558).

3. See Chester, "Retrospective View," 59–66.

4. Reasoner, *Romans*, 70–71.

Romans 7 must be Paul, he argues, because unredeemed people would never say they delight in the law.[5] Augustine adds an important caveat, however. The captivity displayed in this passage is in the apostle's mind and emotions—*not* his actions. Yes, Paul struggled with sin, but he was not subdued by it. Sure, he had sinful desires, but he did not give in to them. Despite the flesh's ferocious call, the apostle still resists the stir of desire and refuses to act upon its urges. In short, for Augustine, though Paul's body was marked by temptation, his deeds were not.

In sermon 151, for example, Augustine explains that the apostle did not lament because he was constrained by lust. Rather, Paul groaned because he grieved even the temptation to sin. To capture his meaning, Augustine paraphrases the apostle by having him confess that what he means is "he does not want to *desire* to covet." Despite this unwanted passion, Augustine's Paul insists in the paraphrase: "I do not consent to this lust."[6] This coincides with what Augustine expands upon elsewhere regarding how all the apostles practiced self-control and did not give in to depraved desires. He clarifies: they still groaned like the wretch, but it was because they wanted to be completely rid of fleshly passions and had grown weary of having to tame them.

Following this, Augustine concludes that Paul's description of himself here is *not* meant to demonstrate that believers are unable to do good, to obey God, and to follow the law. Instead, Augustine infers, believers just cannot do so "perfectly."[7] In other words, Christians are able to do good things—just not flawlessly. In this manner, for him, Romans 7 demonstrates that believers are free to refuse sin but not free from the temptation

---

5. Augustine, "A Treatise against Two Letters of the Pelagians," *NPNF* 1/5:24.

6. Augustine, "Treatise," 24.

7. This interpretation may be influenced by Augustine's reliance on the Latin translation of 7:18 in which because of sin, the *ego* is not able to "perfect" (*perficere*) his deeds.

to sin. But, Augustine concludes, "with the Spirit's help, sin can be resisted and the law fulfilled."[8]

2.2. MARTIN LUTHER: PARDONED BUT NOT UNTETHERED

Martin Luther (1483–1546), an Augustinian monk no less, follows Augustine in considering the *I* in Romans 7 to be the apostle speaking in his own name, "as a spiritual person and not at all as a carnal one."[9] For Luther, the captive represents the whole person, the "*totus-homo*," who paradoxically coexists as both a justified believer and anemic sinner. He goes on to explain: "One and the same man is spiritual and carnal, righteous and sinful, good and evil."[10] Had Luther known modern literary characters, he might say that a believer is simultaneously Jekyll and Hyde, Smeagol and Gollum, or—for the comic book fans—Dr. Osborn and Green Goblin. Any of these would have been better than the distasteful way Luther actually explains his view: for him, our godly mind is like a man and our weak flesh is like a woman. He writes: "Therefore we are the woman because of the flesh, that is, we are carnal, and we are the man because of the spirit which yields to the flesh, we are at the same time both dead and set free."[11]

---

8. Augustine, "Treatise," 24. See Stephen Westerholm, *Perspectives Old and New on Paul: The Lutheran Paul and His Critics* (Grand Rapids: Eerdmans, 2004), 14; Bounds, "Augustine's Interpretation," 15–27.

9. Luther, *Lectures on Romans*, LW 25:200. Luther may be the biggest influencer for the Totally Paul view popular today. To borrow from William Wrede, the transposing of the "soul-strivings of Luther" back onto Paul here has sufficiently colored our portrait of the apostle. William Wrede, *Paul* (London: Green, 1907), 146.

10. Luther, *Lectures on Romans*, 204.

11. Luther, *Lectures on Romans*, 333; WA 56:343.13–16. See also Reasoner, *Romans*, 76.

Luther has a famous catchphrase to describe the condition, *simul iustus et peccator,* "simultaneously saint and sinner."[12] For him, while "sin is forgiven in baptism, so far as condemnation is concerned, it remains in us as a reality, moving us to sin."[13] His argument begins with how the *I* deplores the flesh but loves the law. According to Luther, a carnal man, in contrast to the *ego,* laughs at the law instead of delighting in it. And, rather than fighting sin, he yields and consents to it. Thus, unlike the captive in Romans 7, the carnal person does not even know the evil within him, much less resist it. Instead, afflicted with "sin-fever," the unbeliever "lets himself be carried away by evil and follows it along," all the while considering the law "bitter and harsh and utterly hateful."[14]

In other words, for Luther, the only law the carnal person serves is the law of sin. So, while the unredeemed person, "as everyone knows," surrenders to sinful passions without complaint, Paul, the *I* in this passage, puts up a fight.[15] And, whereas lost people do not recognize their wretchedness and do not long to be delivered from their lusts, the *I*-figure has to be the apostle because "he sighs and grieves and longs to be delivered."[16] And, Luther surmises, only a spiritual man would declare himself wretched in the first place.

Luther clarifies, however, that when Paul says he does evil, the apostle both does it and does not do it. "Inasmuch as he [Paul] resists the evil, it is not his whole person who sins, but only a part of his person."[17] In this strange case, then, Paul's

---

12. Martin Luther, *Commentary on Romans* (Grand Rapids: Kregel, 1982), 99.

13. Luther, *Commentary on Romans,* 100.

14. Luther, *Lectures on Romans,* 207.

15. Luther, *Lectures on Romans,* 207.

16. Luther, *Lectures on Romans,* 208.

17. Luther, *Commentary on Romans,* 97.

Jekyll is blameless, but not his Hyde. Luther also goes on to conclude: "It is indeed a great consolation to us to learn that such a great apostle was involved in the same grievings and afflictions in which we find ourselves when we wish to be obedient to God!"[18] From this perspective, the consolation prize for losing to sin is that Paul did not win against it either. In our misery we enjoy the apostle's company.[19]

Like Augustine, though, Luther makes a significant qualification: Paul does not mean exactly what he says here. Luther elaborates: "We must *not* think that the apostle wants us to understand his statement that he actually does the evil he hates and that he fails to do the good he wants to do."[20] Whereas this may seem to be the meaning of Paul's phrase "to ordinary human understanding," what the apostle was actually saying is that "he does not do the good *as often* and *to such an extent* and *as readily* as he would like."[21] Against the plain reading of the passage, for Luther, Paul's frustration is *not* that he is unable to keep himself from doing bad things or that is he powerless to do the good things he desires. Rather, Luther's Paul remains in agony because "he wants to act from utter single-mindedness, freedom, and cheerfulness, unmolested by the resistance of the flesh, and this he cannot do."[22] Considering this line of reasoning, Luther argues more against the notion of perfectionism than for the bare inability of the believer to do any good.

---

18. Luther, *Lectures on Romans,* 208.

19. Luther adds another odd point: sin actually benefits us by remaining within us. With overpowering sin, we have a chance to exercise ourselves in grace and put off our pride (Luther, *Commentary on Romans*, 100).

20. Luther, *Lectures on Romans*, 203 (emphasis added).

21. Luther, *Lectures on Romans*, 203 (emphasis added).

22. Luther, *Lectures on Romans*, 203.

Speaking of perfectionism, in this discussion, Luther calls out his rival theologians. Fangs bared, he snaps at the so-called great scholars who read much and abound in many books because they do not understand what it means to be a Christian. In their ignorance, they regard it as absurd that Paul, a converted, baptized, spiritual man, "speak of himself as carnal."[23] In contradistinction to these opponents, Luther declares that the apostle describes himself in Romans 7 to show what it means to be a believer: pardoned for sins but not untethered from them.[24]

2.3. JOHN CALVIN: LES MISÉRABLES

John Calvin (1509–1564) falls much in line with Augustine and Luther on this subject, concluding that what the I-figure says in the chapter "cannot be applied to any but to the regenerate." As with Augustine and Luther, Calvin also marshals Romans 7 against his enemies whose philosophy made them far too optimistic about the human condition, causing them to overestimate a person's capacity for freewill. According to Calvin, these nitwits don't realize that "nothing has remained in the heart of man but corruption." Even the best works of the godly "are always stained with some blots of sin," and even the most pious mind that desires to stand "falls, or at least it staggers."[25]

In Calvin's appraisal, while unbelievers are fully depraved, Christians are divided into two portions: one part grace and the other part "relics of the flesh." Thus, for Calvin, the wretch behind the mask is a Christian discouraged with the residue of

---

23. Luther, *Lectures on Romans*, 198.

24. Luther, *Lectures on Romans*, 198.

25. John Calvin, *Commentaries on the Epistle of Paul the Apostle to the Romans*, trans. and ed. John Owen (Edinburgh: Calvin Translation Society, 1849), 265.

the sinful nature, "panting and almost fainting, because he does not find immediate help." The wretch's agonizing cry comes because "no ordinary exercise of divine power" can deliver him from depravity. While Calvin admits that the unregenerate has been known to express similar sentiments to what the *ego* blurts, he insists their groans don't count since their motivation is different than that of the believer. He explains, the lament by Paul is "not to be understood to be the same with what we have heard exists in the ungodly" because, in contrast to the unbeliever, "the godly man consents to the law with the real and most cheerful desire of his heart; for he wishes nothing more than to mount up to heaven."[26]

Calvin asserts that, like the *I* here in Romans 7, when Christians "thoroughly examine themselves, they find in their own nature nothing but misery." He continues: "Paul, by his own example, stimulates them to anxious groanings, and bids them, as long as they sojourn on earth, to desire death, as the only true remedy to their evils."[27] Calvin concludes that the apostle writes Romans 7 to teach us "that we are not only to struggle with our flesh, but also, with continual groaning, to bewail within ourselves and before God our unhappy condition." For Calvin, "this passage is indeed remarkably fitted for the purpose of beating down all the glory of the flesh," since, as illustrated here, even the most perfect among us, so long as they live, "are exposed to misery."[28]

---

26. Calvin, *Romans*, 273.

27. Calvin, *Romans*, 273.

28. Calvin, *Romans*, 273.

2.4. CONCLUSION

As mentioned above, the Totally Paul camp insists the comments in Romans 7 fail to fit the tone of an unbeliever because, for them, the unregenerate person can only bask in sin and not battle against it—much less delight in the law and desire to do good. For this reason, these proponents infer that Paul must be talking about himself as a believer. As we said, it is important to keep in mind that Augustine, Luther, and Calvin all interpret Romans 7 primarily with a pastoral agenda to refute their opponents who argued for some sort of perfectionism. More than from an investigation of the text, they based their conclusions regarding the identity of the *I* on their doctrine of humanity's deep-seated sinfulness in an effort to win a theological debate. This does not devalue their interpretations outright, since they provide a reminder that any believer on this side of glory can still fall to sin.[29] Nonetheless it remains important to recognize that their "far from perfect" campaign in which they interpret Romans 7 differs significantly from the context for which Paul writes Romans 7. So, to borrow from Ben Witherington, their interpretations probably represent an overreaction to their opponents so that they tell us more about these individuals than the concerns of a "rhetorically adept first-century Jewish Christian like Paul."[30]

Contemporary proponents of both the Not Paul and the Totally Paul view owe much to the predecessors of their camps. In comparison to the Not Paul proponents who underline the believers' liberated life in Christ, the Totally Paul interpretation has led many to hold that, though forgiven, believers cannot get

---

29. For more on this, see our section on 1 Cor 10 in ch. 5.

30. Witherington, *Romans*, 188.

past their past.[31] A critical difference separating the two groups today regards their estimation of human depravity. The Not Paul interpreters remain convinced that God's salvation delivers believers from the bondage of sin, so that the wretch sold under sin must be an unbeliever. On the other hand, Totally Paul theologians figure that the "too, too sullied flesh" goes so deep that, even though believers are now in Christ, the specter of their former sin not only still haunts them: it rules, enslaves, and binds them. For them, sin occupies a branch office in our flesh and commandeers our will, pulling the strings of our body like a puppeteer.[32]

To be fair, Augustine and Luther provide nuances that do not often make it to the pulpit or inform the popular view.[33] That is, for these two interpretors, the *ego*'s cry does not actually concern his giving in to sin and doing evil. According to them, the *I can* in fact do good and resist evil. The captive's actual grievance is just that he is tired of dealing with the temptation to sin (Augustine) or that he is frustrated because the good he does is imperfect (Luther).[34]

---

31. To quote my student Austin Knight, "When I was a 'Totally Paul' guy, I used to read Romans 7 and pray that my past ain't ahead of me, but now that I understand the 'Not Paul' view I realize my future ain't what it used to be."

32. David E. Garland, *Romans: An Introduction and Commentary*, TNTC 6 (Downers Grove, IL: InterVarsity Press, 2021), 246–50.

33. Some modern scholars who resist totally ruling out Paul as the wretch also make comments that separate them from the mainstream view and prohibit a reading that provides a believer with an "excuse for persistent moral defeat." James D. G. Dunn, *Romans*, 2 vols., WBC 38 (Waco, TX: Word, 1988), 1:412. See also Will N. Timmins, *Romans 7 and Christian Identity: A Study of the "I" in Its Literary Context*, SNTSMS 170 (Cambridge: Cambridge University Press, 2017), 8; and Thomas R. Schreiner, *Romans*, 2nd ed., BECNT (Grand Rapids: Baker Academic, 2018), 390.

34. Calvin likely lines up with Luther here considering his comment above regarding how even the best works of the godly "are always stained with some blots of sin." See Westerholm, *Perspectives*, 60.

With all this said, the goal of the last two chapters has been to give a brief history of a long, complicated debate. We delineated two oversimplified interpretive options: the Not Paul view versus the Totally Paul view. We have tried to give a fair hearing to both sides, even though we already admitted in the introduction that we believe the *I*-figure's statements contradict what Paul says everywhere else about how the Holy Spirit enables believers to overcome sin. In the interests of transparency, our view falls in between these two poles. We think Paul is mostly talking about himself *before he met Christ* in order to spell out the relationship between the law and sin as well as to sound a warning to anyone trying to achieve freedom through the law rather than by the Spirit. We will explain this reading in chapter 8. First, however, we endeavor to discount the popular interpretation that depicts Paul and mature believers as helpless captives to the power of sin.

As in the last chapter, we thought we would include a table to highlight four major arguments for the Totally Paul view in case you need a reference point later on. Again, we will go into more depth on these and others later in the book (see esp. chs. 6–7).

The *I* must be Paul because:

1. He desires to keep God's law, which is uncharacteristic for an unbeliever.

2. He declares himself *wretched* which only a spiritual man would do.

3. He gives thanks to God, who delivered him through Christ.

4. He describes the common Christian experience of constant misery resulting from becoming more conscious of sin as one matures in the faith.

3 ～

The *I* of the Storm

A Walk-Through of Romans 5–8

Once at a Fourth of July barbeque in Queens, with my heart as full of patriotism as my belly was with food, I began belting out Bruce Springsteen's "Born in the U.S.A." My friend Daniel interrupted me and said, "You know that song is actually criticizing America." I didn't believe him, so he pulled up the lyrics on his phone to show me the context surrounding the famous chorus. Sure enough, the song depicts the United States as a country that kicks her people when they're down, so that they live their days like a battered dog bracing for a blow. Shamefaced, I realized that I had neglected the context of the chorus and had therefore read my own national pride into a heartsick lament about how so many born in the U.S.A. deserve so much better than what they're getting. Whether it's a 1984 rock song by the Boss or a first-century letter by the apostle, context determines meaning. Since all of us (whether we are in the Not Paul or Totally Paul group) have interpretive lenses smeared with the fingerprints of our tradition, a concentrated examination of the original literary context exists as a crucial first step for understanding any passage, especially one as rife with controversy as Romans 7.

Paul, an intentional and skillful writer, intends for us to follow the flow and structure of his argument so as to be able to trace out his meaning. To this end, interpreters on both sides of the argument tend to divide Romans up into four main blocks, with chapters 1–4 focused more on justification by faith, chapters 5–8 on sanctification through the Spirit, chapters 9–11 on the status of Israel, and chapters 12–15 on the ethical implications of the gospel. Since most scholars consider Romans 5 to be a transition from chapters 1–4 to chapters 5–8, we will start there.

Grant Osborne proposes that Romans 5–8 forms a familiar A-B-C-C-B-A pattern.[1] It looks something like this:

> A Results of justification: God's love and Spirit in suffering and the assurance of glory (5:1–11)
>
>> B Basis for assurance: life in the new Adam (5:12–21)
>>
>>> C Freedom from sin and the law (6:1–23)
>>>
>>> C' Freedom from the law and sin (7:1–25)
>>
>> B' Basis for assurance: new life in the Spirit (8:1–16)
>
> A' Results of justification: glory and assurance in the Spirit, God's love in suffering (8:17–39)

---

1. Grant Osborne, "The Flesh without the Spirit: Romans 7 and Christian Experience," in Wilder, *Perspectives on Our Struggle*, 7. See also Douglas J. Moo, *Romans*, NICNT (Grand Rapids: Eerdmans, 1996), 294. I have modified his presentation.

Beginning and ending with the *A*s in the structure, Paul stresses the results of salvation for those justified by faith. He proclaims that believers have hope in suffering and the assurance of redemption because of God's love in Christ through the Spirit (5:1–11). On the other end of the structure (*A'*), the apostle declares that, as divine heirs, believers share in both glory and suffering. Paul then expounds upon the ministry of the Spirit and the constancy of divine love no matter what afflictions his followers might face (8:17–39).[2]

The two *B*s on the diagram provide the basis for assurance. Jesus, the Second Adam, has overturned the failings of the first man, so that now, instead of sin and death, believers have certainty of holiness and life (5:12–21). Moreover, those who walk according to the Spirit have a new life in which they fulfill the righteous requirement of the law (8:1–13). Finally, the *C*s, where our passage falls, asserts that Christ-followers are free from sin so that they no longer live under it as their master (6:1–23), and, on the other side, that they are also liberated from the law so that they belong to the Lord (7:1–25). With this overarching structure in place, we are better suited to walk through these passages in more depth.

3.1. A. RESULTS OF JUSTIFICATION (5:1–11)

In Romans 5:1, Paul announces that believers have peace with God and access to him because they have been justified by faith. The apostle assures his readers they also have a boast in the hope of future glory and in the face of present suffering. He goes

---

2. Paul ends 5:1 with the phrase "through our Lord Jesus Christ" and 8:39 with "in Christ Jesus our Lord." Frank Thielman, *Romans*, ZECNT (Grand Rapids: Zondervan, 2018), 364.

on to expand what he means by this. When Christ-followers endure affliction, they gain a godly character and grasp a certain hope—knowing God will never give them up, let them down, run away, or desert them. Believers can count on this since the Spirit has poured his love into their hearts. Even when his people were frail, sinful, and weak, the Lord demonstrated this love by sending his Son to die for them. Since God saved them in the past through the blood of Jesus, they can be confident he will also deliver them in the future through the life of Christ. And, because believers are reconciled to him, they have a boast, a shout of triumph. They can boast not only because God has saved them and because he will save them, but also because right here, right now, they have reconciliation with him. In other words, what the Lord is doing in their present life is evidence of what he did in their past and proof of what he will do in their future.

3.2. *B.* BASIS FOR ASSURANCE: LIFE IN THE NEW ADAM (5:12–21)

Next, Paul takes the audience all the way back to Adam, through whom the powers of sin and death entered the world and reigned over humanity. According to the apostle, the previous fate and miserable condition of believers were tied to the first man. But then, the Second Adam came; his name is Jesus. He promptly reversed the curse by obeying where the first man did not. As a result, God's righteousness and grace have uncrowned sin and dethroned death. And, in contrast to the resulting condemnation of Adam's epic fail, Christ's decisive act of obedience and overflowing righteousness brought justification and life. So, for believers, where sin abounds, grace superabounds.

3.3. C. FREEDOM FROM SIN AND
THE LAW (ROMANS 6:1–23)

In Romans 6, Paul returns to his pattern of asking rhetorical questions to delineate his theology and press his point. "Should we continue to sin, then, so that grace may abound?" (6:2 NASB). The apostle follows this inconceivable notion with a strong "absolutely not!" He reasons:

1. Christ died to sin once and for all.

2. We died with Christ through baptism.

3. Therefore, we too are dead to sin so that we should live a new life.[3]

This new life in Christ no longer continues in sin, cowers before the flesh, or complies to its desires, for, through baptism, believers were crucified with the Lord so that their bodies are no longer captives to iniquity. Having died with Christ, his followers should live with Christ. And, just as the Lord died to sin so that he lives to God, so also, believers should count themselves dead to sin and alive to God in Christ Jesus.

Paul goes on to accentuate the truth that God is their master and sin is not. To prevent his readers from missing this promise, he repeats himself to the point of being superfluous and redundant. Once again, he underscores how those redeemed by grace do not live under the law and should not, under any circumstances, let sin reign in them. Those in Christ must cease and desist from obeying sin's desires and from offering their body parts to it as instruments for wickedness and as weapons against righteousness. Paul then fires off another rhetorical question: "Shall we sin because we are not under the law but

---

3. Moo, *Romans*, 354n12.

under grace?" (6:15). His answer is another resounding "No!" A person is a slave to whichever master they serve. In this case, as Jesus also concluded in the Sermon on the Mount, people can only have one master. The choice of lords, according to Paul, is sin who leads to death or obedience resulting in righteousness. To remove all doubt, Paul proclaims that the church's allegiance is to the Lord. Sin is the *former* master, with whom believers should never ever get back together.

Based on this breakup, the apostle adjures the church to offer themselves as fully to godliness and holiness as they used to offer themselves to impurity and wickedness. As if the apostle cannot repeat himself enough, he declares again that the believer has been set free from sin and has become a slave to God. For this reason, Christ-followers now have present holiness and everlasting life. Paul punctuates the chapter with the familiar verse, sounding both a warning shot and a promise for the church: "The wages of sin is death, but the gift of God is eternal life in Christ Jesus our Lord" (6:23).

For those keeping score, the chart below demonstrates how often Paul says in Romans 6 that the believer is set free from sin and should no longer live in it.

We are those who have died to sin; how can we live in it any longer? (6:2)

For we know that our old self was crucified with him so that the body ruled by sin might be done away with, that we should no longer be slaves to sin—because anyone who has died has been set free from sin. (6:6–7)

Count yourselves dead to sin but alive to God in Christ Jesus. (6:11)

Do not let sin reign in your mortal body so that you obey its evil desires. (6:12)

Do not offer any part of yourself to sin as an instrument of wickedness. (6:13)

Sin shall no longer be your master. (6:14)

Shall we sin because we are not under the law but under grace? By no means! (6:15)

Though you used to be slaves to sin, you have come to obey from your heart the pattern of teaching that has now claimed your allegiance. (6:17)

You have been set free from sin and have become slaves to righteousness. (6:18)

Just as you used to offer yourselves as slaves to impurity and to ever-increasing wickedness, so now offer yourselves as slaves to righteousness leading to holiness. (6:19)

When you were slaves to sin, you were free from the control of righteousness. (6:20)

But now that you have been set free from sin and have become slaves of God, the benefit you reap leads to holiness, and the result is eternal life. (6:22)

This recurring liberation theme is important when seeking to identify the wretch who claims to remain captive to sin in Romans 7. Another key tool in this venture is to notice how Paul uses the rhetorical questions in his argument in 6:1 and 6:15, since he continues this sequence in 7:7 and 7:13.

3.4. C′. FREEDOM FROM THE LAW AND SIN (ROMANS 7:1–25)

3.4.1. ROMANS 7:1–6

In 7:1, Paul focuses on a more particular audience: "those who know the law." Everywhere else in the letter, Paul refers to his Jewish kinsfolk as those who received the law (2:17; 3:2; 9:4) while distinguishing gentiles as those absent of it (2:14).[4] Because of this, the passage likely addresses Jewish believers, and/or gentile Christians with a background in the synagogue and training in the law.[5] While this specific address does not rule out an application of Romans 7 for the other gentile Christians,[6] Paul concerns himself here with an audience involved in Torah.[7]

As we mentioned above, Romans 6 and 7 contain parallels to highlight how the gospel both liberated believers from sin and unfettered them from the law. For instance, Paul starts Romans 6 with a "Do you not know?" statement (v. 3) to stress

---

4. McKnight identifies this group with the so-called weak believers in Rom 14–15 whose conviction is culturally shaped by Torah observance. Scot McKnight, *Reading Romans Backwards* (Waco, TX: Baylor University Press, 2019), 160.

5. See Kyle B. Wells, *Grace and Agency in Paul and Second Temple Judaism: Interpreting the Transformation of the Heart*, NovTSup 157 (Leiden: Brill, 2015), 240; and Collin G. Kruse, *Paul's Letter to the Romans*, PNTC (Grand Rapids, Eerdmans, 2012), 305.

6. E.g., having begun with the Spirit, they should not try to finish with the law (see Gal 3:3).

7. Brian Dodd, *Paul's Paradigmatic "I": Personal Example as Literary Strategy*, JSNTSup 177 (Sheffield: Sheffield Academic, 1999), 222.

how those who were baptized into the death of Christ have been set free from sin so as to walk in the newness of life. The apostle begins Romans 7 with the same "Do you not know?" This time, he does so to explain how those familiar with the law have, through Christ, died to the law so that they are released from the old way of the letter and now walk in the newness of the Spirit.[8]

Romans 6	Romans 7
Don't you know that all of us who were baptized into Christ Jesus were baptized into his death?	*Do you not know* … that the law has authority over someone only as long as that person lives?
We were therefore *buried with him through baptism*	So, my brothers and sisters, *you also died to the law through the body of Christ*
just as Christ *was raised from the dead* through the glory of the Father	to him *who was raised from the dead*
we too may live a new life	we serve in the new way of the Spirit
the fruit you reap leads to holiness	in order that we might bear fruit for God

8. Cf. John Stott, *Romans: God's Good News for the World* (Downers Grove, IL: InterVarsity Press, 1994), 189.

John Stott also provides a helpful comparison.[9]

Romans 6:1–23	Romans 7:1–4
We died to sin.	We died to the law.
We died to sin in union with Christ's death.	We died to the law through the body of Christ.
We have been freed from sin.	We have been released from the law.
We share in Christ's resurrection.	We belong to him who was raised from the dead.
We now live in newness of life.	We now serve in the newness of the Spirit.
We bear fruit that leads to holiness.	We bear fruit to God.

To illustrate this point, Paul begins Romans 7 with the hypothetical situation of a married woman having sex with another man. Legally this would be considered an illicit affair, but if the woman is a widow, she is released from the law and allowed to remarry. In this parable, the widow represents the believer who, because of death, is free from her previous covenant. With respect to this liberating death, however, Paul makes an unexpected shift. Rather than a deceased husband, Paul depicts the

---

9. Stott, *Romans*, 194.

woman (the believer) as the one who has died so that she might belong to her new man, the risen Christ. Newly married, she no longer produces for death; instead, she bears fruit to God. Paul's metaphorical language can make his line of reasoning seem confusing here. His point, however, follows the one he made in Romans 6. Through participation in Christ's death, believers have died to both sin and the law so that they are free to walk and serve in the Spirit with holiness and obedience (7:5–6).[10]

Scholars tend to agree that 7:5–6 give the outline for what Paul is going to explain in 7:7–8:11.[11] In short, the problem of one's defeat to sin under the law, which 7:5 points to, is solved by the presence of the Spirit in the believer's life, which 7:6 points to. Therefore, 7:5 serves as the heading for 7:7–25, representing the wretched life replete with sin, flesh, and death.

> For when we were in the realm of the flesh, the sinful passions aroused by the law were at work in us, so that we bore fruit for death. (7:5)

Romans 7:6, on the other hand, looks forward to what the apostle will unpack in 8:1–11, elucidating the new life marked with the Spirit, freedom, righteousness, and peace.

> But now, by dying to what once bound us, we have been released from the law so that we serve in the new way of the Spirit, and not in the old way of the written code. (7:6)

---

10. See Bruce W. Longenecker, "Sin and the Sovereignty of God in Romans," in *Sin and Its Remedy in Paul*, ed. Nijay K. Gupta and John K. Goodrich (Eugene, OR: Cascade, 2020), 47–48.

11. Cf. Stefano Romanello, "Rom 7,7–25 and the Impotence of the Law: A Fresh Look at a Much-Debated Topic Using Literary-Rhetorical Analysis" *Bib* 84 (2003): 510–30.

Thomas Schreiner conveys it like this:[12]

| Life under the law in the flesh (7:5) | → | Life under the law in the flesh elaborated (7:7–25) |
| Life in the Spirit (7:6) | → | Life in the Spirit elaborated (8:1–17) |

Considering this outline, Krister Stendahl comments that as Paul goes into the monologue of the wretch, 7:5–6 provide proof the audience already has an awareness of the solution to the dilemma the apostle is about to detail in 7:7–25.[13]

This antithesis in 7:5–6 as well as Paul's language of enslaved captivity under sin in 7:14 lead many scholars to reject the Totally Paul view.[14] They also note that the distinct absence of the Holy Spirit in the wretch's deliberations serves another critical point against the popular view, especially in comparison to Romans 8 wherein the Spirit is mentioned over twenty times with no hint of despair or defeat to sin.[15] The lack of reference to the Spirit in 7:7–25 makes it seem that the poor, outmatched creature is all on their own against the wiles of evil.

Since Paul could have seamlessly continued his train of thought from 7:6 to 8:1, most scholars consider 7:7–25 a

---

12. Schreiner, *Romans*, 378. Arrows added.

13. Krister Stendahl, "The Apostle Paul and the Introspective Conscience of the West," *HTR* 56:3 (1963): 213.

14. E.g., Barclay, *Paul*, 502n14.

15. Gordon D. Fee, *God's Empowering Presence: The Holy Spirit in the Letters of Paul* (Peabody, MA: Hendrickson, 1994), 514.

parenthesis to, or an excursion from, the apostle's major line of reasoning.[16] But, if so, why does Paul need a detour here?

3.4.2. ROMANS 7:7–13

The apostle now seeks to explain the potentially disparaging things he has written about the law so far. At first glance, Paul appears to have placed the law on the same opposing team as sin, flesh, and death. For instance, he previously wrote about how the law sneaked in the back door to increase trespasses (5:20).[17] He then placed the law over against God's grace: "Shall we sin because we are not under the law but under grace?" (6:15). In other words, the reason sin is *not* the church's boss is because believers are not under the law. This comment coheres with his statement regarding how the law arouses sinful passions within people (7:5). It is one thing to say the law failed to bring about salvation from sin, but Paul ups the ante by arguing that the law even stirs sin up. Somehow for the apostle being under the law facilitates the reign of sin. He needs to explain.

Many scholars infer that the apostle writes the rest of Romans 7 to defend his view of the law and to come to its defense.[18] Of this, Jarvis Williams writes: "The fundamental focus of the text is not to convey Paul's personal experience, but to emphasize that sin uses the law to produce death."[19] Thus, the apostle does not seek to answer questions about Christian

---

16. Chester, "Retrospective View," 80.

17. See Joseph R. Dodson, *The "Powers" of Personification: Rhetorical Purpose in the "Book of Wisdom" and the Letter to the Romans*, BZNW 161 (Berlin: de Gruyter, 2008), 143–45.

18. Cf. Joshua W. Jipp, "Educating the Divided Soul in Paul and Plato: Reading Romans 7:7–25 and Plato's Republic," in *Paul: Jew, Greek, and Roman*, ed. Stanley Porter, Pauline Studies 5 (Leiden: Brill, 2008), 231–57.

19. Jarvis Williams, *One New Man: The Cross and Racial Reconciliation in Pauline Theology* (Nashville: B&H Academic, 2010), 48.

holiness here. As Stott puts it: the passage is more historical than personal; it is Paul "struggling with the place of the law in God's purpose."[20] So, in 7:7–25, the apostle explains that the law is not wicked, just weak. Moreover, "the law is part of the dilemma not despite being holy, but precisely because it is."[21] In other words, although the law is righteous and good, it is powerless to overcome sin. Stronger than the law, sin hijacks the law and manipulates it. Thereby, sin stimulates the desires of those under the law so as to kill and capture them. So, to draw from Chang, whereas 6:1–7:6 demonstrates what *Christ can do* (i.e., liberate a person from sin), 7:7–25 demonstrates what *the law cannot do* (i.e., liberate a person from sin).[22]

As Paul used rhetorical questions in 6:1 and 6:15 to help the reader get his point, he follows the same sequence in 7:7 and 7:13, asking "Does this mean the law is sin?" and "Did that which is good, then, become death to me?" To both he answers: "Most certainly not!" First, the law is not sin because it helps a person understand what sin is; and second, the law did not bring about death but results in death so that sin might be exposed for its perversity. In short, the law unmasks sin and gives it recognizable definition so as to remove ambiguity from the sinful act.[23]

Considering these two statements, the apostle would have probably approved of John Bunyan's allegorical illustration of the law. In *Pilgrim's Progress,* the main character named Christian is led into a room that had never been swept. Then another figure called Interpreter beckons a man to come sweep

20. Stott, *Romans,* 189.

21. Leander E. Keck, *Romans,* ANTC (Nashville: Abingdon, 2005), 179.

22. Chang, "Life," 279.

23. Dunn, *Romans,* 1:386.

the floor causing the dust to stir so much Christian almost chokes to death. Rightly startled, Christian asks Interpreter why he did that. Interpreter explains that the room represents the heart of an unbeliever, and the dirt, original sin and inward corruption that had thoroughly defiled him. Interpreter continues: the broom, on the other hand, signifies the law, which caused the hidden dust to swirl about but making it more difficult to clean. Interpreter then spells it out: "This is to show you that the Law, instead of it effectively cleansing the heart from sin, does in fact arouse, give greater strength to, and cause sin to flourish in the soul." This suffocating result, Interpreter concludes, rises from the truth that though "the Law both uncovers and condemns sin," it does not have "the power to subdue it." (What is needed to vanquish sin is a washbucket not a broom, cue Romans 8.)[24]

Instead of allegorical figures, a dirty room, and a broom, Paul instantiates how the law works to expose sin's true character by switching to the first-person singular and appealing to the "do not covet" prohibition given to Israel at Sinai. He writes: "I did not even know what coveting was until the law told me not to covet." Paul's rationale is the law cannot be sin because it reveals sin. He continues, "While I myself was formerly alive outside of the law," sin, in a surprising twist, sprang to life at the coming of the command. Subsequently, it used this command as a base of operations to deceive and kindle "every kind of coveting" within the wretch (7:8, 11). And, through this holy and righteous commandment meant for life, sin produced death in him. Therefore, sin—*not the law*—remains the real culprit for bringing death into the world.

---

24. John Bunyan, *Pilgrim's Progress* (New York: Hurst, 1903), 110–11.

Here we arrive at 7:14–25, the persnickety passage we address in this book. Since the goal of this chapter is setting the context, we will resist tracing out these verses in this chapter and will continue into 8:1–13 instead.

3.5. B'. BASIS FOR ASSURANCE: NEW LIFE IN THE SPIRIT (8:1–13)

Chapters and verses were not in the original biblical text and can sometimes influence our interpretation of a passage. So, just as it is beneficial to place Romans 7 side-by-side with Romans 6 to see the continuity of Paul's thought regarding the church's freedom from sin and the law, readers should remember that the argument in Romans 7 does not actually end in Romans 7 but extends to Romans 8.

Jason Maston has shown how 7:7–25 is the negative counterpart to 8:1–13.[25] The contrast here, to borrow from Preston Sprinkle, lies between the powerlessness of the law to give life in Romans 7 and the power of God to do so in Romans 8.[26] In this juxtaposition, what was impossible for the wretch hampered by the flesh is now possible for the believer empowered by the Spirit. In other words, according to Paul, people needed to be released from the law because it, like the *ego*, cannot resist sin. In fact, if the law could speak, it would harmonize with the wretch: "Hey man, what I [the law] wanted to do I could not do either, and when I tried to do good, sin was right there with me too. You say it is not you, but it's not me either. Sin's in charge!" The apostle does go on to redeem the law. For Paul, the law fulfilled its purpose. Having exposed sin as vulgar, baleful, and

---

25. Jason Maston, *Divine and Human Agency in Second Temple Judaism and Paul: A Comparative Study*, WUNT 2/297 (Tübingen: Mohr Siebeck, 2010), 130.

26. Preston Sprinkle, *Law and Life: The Interpretation of Leviticus 18:5 in Early Judaism and in Paul*, WUNT 2/241 (Tübingen: Mohr Siebeck, 2008), 188.

vile, the law's goal is completed. And its job of pointing to Christ is done (cf. 10:4).

Over against the frustration and self-denigration of the *I*, Paul proclaims in 8:1 that there is *now* no condemnation for those who are in Christ Jesus, those whom the Spirit has set free from the law of sin and death. In the words of Dunn, "Paul makes very clear that there are *two foundations of new life* for the believer. The first is what God has done in Christ: he has dealt with sin in effect by loading it on Christ." The second, Dunn continues, is "the action of the Spirit," whose power is greater than the power of sin.[27]

Regarding the first foundation: the apostle explains that through the incarnate Christ, God did what the good-yet-weak law could not. The Lord condemned sin in the flesh so that the righteous requirement of the law would be fulfilled within believers. Unlike the miserable creature, Christ-followers walk according to the Spirit. For Paul, the role of the Spirit is so important, he defines the believer in terms of it. Stated negatively: anyone who does not have the Spirit does not belong to God (8:9). Stated positively: all who are led by the Spirit are children of God (8:14).[28] Because of the Lord and his Spirit, no reason remains for believers to continue "in a life of penal servitude," bound to carry out the dictates of the tyranny of sin.[29] Since the law of the Spirit of life in Christ Jesus is stronger than indwelling sin, it profoundly sets his people free. Whereas Romans 8 begins with "no condemnation" and ends with "no

---

27. James D. G. Dunn, "The Balance of Already/Not Yet: Romans 8:1–17," in *Preaching Romans: Four Perspectives*, ed. Scot McKnight and Joseph B. Modica (Grand Rapids, Eerdmans, 2019), 102, emphasis original.

28. Dunn, "Balance," 102.

29. F. F. Bruce, *The Epistle of Paul to the Romans: An Introduction and Commentary*, TNTC (Grand Rapids: Eerdmans, 1985), 159.

separation" for believers, in between there is "no defeat" for them either.[30] The sin that had overthrown the wretch has now been overthrown. To quote F. F. Bruce: "with the entry of the Spirit there is no further talk of defeat. The conflict goes on, but where the Spirit is in control the power of … sin is mastered."[31]

In further contrast to the inner turmoil, chaos, and frustration of the *ego*, the new mind of the believer is governed by the Spirit, resulting in a life of peace and self-control. In contradistinction to the blot and blemish of the captive, the Christ-follower is marked by successful submission to God's law. An overarching point of Romans 7–8, then, is that the enslaving power of sin must be replaced by the enabling power of the Spirit.[32] In this vein, Paul continues: those who belong to Christ have the Spirit of Christ so that they no longer live according to the flesh.

Sure, believers' bodies will still die, too; like the flowers of the field, all flesh fades away, including those liberated from sin. Nevertheless, death does not have the last word. The church has the promise of resurrection. The same Spirit who raised the Lord will raise his people too (8:11). As Paul puts it elsewhere, even though "the sting of death is sin, and the power of sin is the law" (1 Cor 15:56), Christ will put death to death so that his followers can taunt it and proclaim:

Where, O death, is your victory?
Where, O death, is your sting? (1 Cor 15:55)

While Christians are all destined to die, this does not mean they are bound to sin. In Romans 8:12–13, Paul immediately clarifies:

---

30. Leon Morris, *The Epistle to the Romans*, PNTC (Grand Rapids: Eerdmans, 1994), 299.

31. Bruce, Romans, 162.

32. Keck, *Romans,* 179.

since believers have God dwelling within them, they no longer have an obligation to sin or to indulge the flesh. Rather, it is their duty to mortify the misdeeds of their bodies so that they will live (8:12–13; cf. 6:23).

3.6. CONCLUSION

In conclusion, from 6:1–23; 7:1–6; and 8:1–13, Paul gives no evidence that believers will continue to be exploited, enslaved, and defeated by sin. There is no mention of remaining helplessly captive to the flesh, unable to do any good. It is emphatically the opposite. Through Christ, believers have not only been set free from the penalty of sin, but in Christ they have also been liberated from its irresistible sway. Romans 7:14–25 remains the misfit here and should therefore be read considering the immediate context that concerns life under the law instead of life in the Lord.

4 ～

The *Eye* behind the *I*

A Brief Exposition of 7:14–25

Anaïs Nin states that we tend not to see texts as they are—because, she explains, "it is the 'I' behind the 'eye' that does the seeing." In order to remove as much of our own *I* behind our reading of Romans 7 and to see the *ego* through the eye of the original audience (as much as possible), we have investigated the literary context of 7:14–25 in the last chapter. From that perspective we saw that this passage follows Paul's explanation of how believers are no longer under the law since they have died with Christ and live by the Spirit (7:1–6). This does not mean, Paul underscores, that the law is sinful. It just did not have the strength to keep sin from using it to ensnare and slaughter those under it (7:7–13). Considering Paul's previous comments, many scholars agree that, in 7:14–25, he defends his view of the law, explaining how sly and fatal sin exploited the good-but-weak law to bring forth the *ego*'s condemnation and death.

If you have your Bible in hand, you can notice that two significant grammatical shifts occur from 7:8–13 to 7:14–25. First,

Paul changes the verb tense to magnify the wretch's experience (we will discuss this more in ch. 6). Second, he moves from sin as the main subject of the verbs to the *I* as the primary subject of them. That is to say, in the former section, Paul focuses on sin as the actor, and the *I*-figure as the passive victim. *Sin* seizes the opportunity of the law; *sin* comes to life; *sin* deceives; *sin* kills. So, sin, as the main subject of 7:9–11, sets the backdrop for the picture Paul paints of the *ego* in 7:14–25. As we will see below, however, Paul also shifts the metaphor from sin as a *murderer* (with the *I* as its *victim*) to sin as the *slave master* (with the *I* as its *prisoner of war*). Sin also strikingly moves from *killing* the wretch to *living* within him. To draw from Eastman, within the wretch, sin works as a hostile colonizing power that inhabits and overtakes them, causing them to act against their own desires and thereby separating the results of their actions from their own intentions.[1]

4.1. BIT BY BIT AND VERSE BY VERSE

4.1.1. ROMANS 7:14–16

> For we know that the law is spiritual, but I myself am fleshly: having been auctioned off as a slave under the power of sin. For I do not understand what I am doing, because I do not practice what I want to do, but I do what I hate. Now if I do what I do not want to do, I agree with the law that it is good. (author's translation)

Paul begins 7:14 with the conjunction "for," referencing his previous conclusion that sin manipulated the law to kill the wretch,

---

1. Eastman, *Paul*, 109–10. For more on this, see Dodson, *"Powers" of Personification*, 123–39.

which served to expose the sinfulness of sin. As if to remind the audience of the in-house nature of the passage, the apostle once more addresses "those who know the law" (see 7:1) before he centers in on the *I* for the rest of the chapter.[2]

In 7:12, Paul underlines the virtue of the law, considering it holy, righteous, and good. So also, here in 7:14, the wretch agrees that the law is "spiritual." As N. T. Wright remarks, in light of the flesh/spirit, Adam/Christ, and slave/free contrasts in the letter, Paul finally places the law on the right side. Sadly for the miserable creature, he remains for the moment fleshly, Adamic, and bound to sin.[3] Now, the problem is not the law but the precarious predicament of the *ego*. When referring to the captive here, Paul uses an emphatic *I* (*autos egō*), which is often employed for contrast and focus. Here it declares how, over against the law, the wretch is unspiritual, and even worse, sold as a slave to sin. The *I*-figure's situation parallels that of the unredeemed people in 3:9–20, who "under the power of sin" also fail to do good and walk in misery and ruin. Like the wretch, these unredeemed sinners in Romans 3 do not know peace, and, as with the miserable creature, the law has spoken to them in order to make them conscious of their sin as well.

As if the emphatic *I* is not enough, Paul also uses a pronounced verb tense here to zoom in, center on, and highlight the wretch's bondage and sinful experience: "*sold* into bondage to sin" (7:14 NASB). The last time Paul used this strong verb tense, he did so to intensify how the one participating in Christ's death has been "*freed* from the bondage of sin" (6:7, emphasis added). The idea the apostle construes here, that a believer is "fleshly" and

---

2. The "we" here may refer to the "weak in faith" in Rom 14–15, who—according to McKnight—stumble over Paul's law-free gospel (McKnight, *Romans*, 160).

3. N. T. Wright, "The Letter to the Romans," *NIB* 10:566.

"sold under sin," contravenes his earlier demand regarding the Christian's release from sin.[4] For Douglas Moo, sin's auctioning off the wretch as a slave settles the argument once and for all and provides decisive proof Paul does not describe a Christian in these verses.[5] Along these lines, Richard Longenecker remarks that if this depiction represents the Christian life, the logical conclusion is that "redemption by Christ is no redemption at all."[6] For this reason, with Moo and Longenecker, many scholars believe the *I* is not Paul referring to himself as a believer.[7]

Depending on how one takes "I am of the flesh" in 7:14 (CSB), the *ego*'s claim may also conflict with what Paul proclaims in 8:9 regarding how believers are no longer in the flesh but in the Spirit.[8]

The Believer	The Wretch
So that we may no longer be enslaved to sin (6:5–7) You are not in the flesh, but in the Spirit (8:9)	I am sold as a slave under sin (7:14) I am of the flesh (7:14)

Paul goes on to demonstrate in Romans 7 how the miserable creature's condition of being fleshly and in bondage results in the *I*-figure's despair, causing him to lament: "I do not

---

4. See Peter Stuhlmacher, *Paul's Letter to the Romans: A Commentary*, trans. S. J. Hafemann (Louisville: Westminster John Knox, 1994), 115.

5. Moo, *Romans*, 454.

6. Richard Longenecker, *The Epistle to the Romans: A Commentary on the Greek Text*, NIGTC (Grand Rapids: Eerdmans, 2016), 621.

7. See C. H. Dodd, *The Epistle of Paul to the Romans*, MNTC (New York: Harper, 1932), 108.

8. Cf. Timmins, *Romans 7*, 66–91, 179.

understand what I do. For what I want to do, I do not do, but what I hate I do" (7:15).

In 7:16, the apostle elucidates one upside to this tragic human situation: when the wretch does what he does not desire to do, it underscores that the law is good. This is at least the fifth compliment Paul lavishes upon the law in this chapter: it is holy, righteous, spiritual, excellent, and good. These praises reinforce the argument that the concern here is to vindicate the law's connection with sin rather than to describe the believer's relationship with the flesh.

4.1.2. ROMANS 7:17–20

So now I am no longer the one doing it, but it is sin living in me. For I know that nothing good lives in me, that is, in my flesh. For the desire to do what is good is with me, but there is no ability to do it. For I do not do the good that I want to do, but I practice the evil that I do not want to do. Now if I do what I do not want, I am no longer the one that does it, but it is the sin that lives in me. (author's translation)

In 7:17, Paul once again uses the emphatic I (*autos egō*), this time to reveal how the wretch's condition is worse than previously imagined. Now the miserable creature is not merely *under* sin: sin lives and works *in* him. In 7:18, the law reveals to the miserable creature an astounding revelation. The captive is no longer the one doing what he hates. It turns out, sin dwelling in him is to blame. It is the culprit, the miscreant, and felon. While Paul has already separated the law from sin, here he separates the self from sin as well.[9]

---

9. De Waal Dryden, "Revisiting Romans 7," 148.

It is not the law, it is sin. (7:9–11)

It is not me, it is sin. (7:14–25)

Although this gesture smacks of the "devil made me do it," for Paul, it is more diabolical than that. Sin does not make the *ego* do bad things; sin itself does bad things within him. In short, sin sins, not the wretch.[10]

But the *ego* has not been completely erased. It still knows, wants, discovers, and delights. As Eastman states: "The person here is described as occupied territory, his subjectivity colonized by an oppressive foreign power, his members mobilized for actions contrary to his deepest wants, but yet he remains cognizant of his loss of freedom." She continues: "He may experience this combination of self-awareness and crippled capacity as inner division, but it is the internalization of sin's lethal embrace."[11]

As he is enfolded in the deadly clutches of sin, the law makes the miserable creature attentive to the cesspool of his flesh, so that he finally sees nothing good dwells within him. Now he understands even more that although his desire to do good is there, his ability to carry out that good is not. So, in 7:19–20, the wretch is back where he started: experiencing the dilemma of not doing the good he desires but doing the evil he does not want to do. Notice the similarities.

---

10. Further, the verbs describing sin's actions here—"doing," "practicing," and "accomplishing"—are those that formerly characterized unredeemed humanity (see 1:32; 2:1–3, 9; 3:8); see Eastman, *Paul*, 110–13.

11. Eastman, *Paul*, 114.

Romans 7:15–17	Romans 7:19–20
I do not practice what I want to do,	I do not do the good that I want to do,
but I do what I hate.	but I do the evil that I do not want to do.
Now if I do what I do not want to do,	Now if I do what I do not want,
I agree with the law that it is good.	I am no longer the one that does it,
… but it is sin living in me.	… but it is the sin that lives in me.

As 7:15–17 and 7:19–20 illustrate, the *ego* repeats itself to establish it is no longer in charge, not even the master of its own house or domain. Like the law, it is helpless in the hands of sin. Try as it may, it just can't compete.

4.1.3. ROMANS 7:21–25

So I discover this law: When I want to do what is good, evil is present with me. For in my inner self I delight in God's law, but I see a different law in the parts of my body, waging war against the law of my mind and taking me prisoner to the law of sin in the parts of my body. What a wretched man I am! Who will rescue me from this body of death? Thanks be to God through Jesus Christ our Lord! So then, with my mind I myself am serving the law of God, but with my flesh, the law of sin. (CSB)

Through this experience, the *I* finds another law at work in him—namely, though he desires to do good, evil is right there with him. No matter how much he delights in the law with his inner man, this other law works in his body. It dwells within his members, wars within his mind, and imprisons his will. These depictions of sin engaging in combat and incarcerating the miserable creature correspond with the earlier remark about his being sold under sin, and they also fit nicely with the other military metaphors recurring in Romans 6.

In response to the debilitating situation, the captive finally cries out, "I am a miserable man!" (7:24). While the word translated "miserable" here often connotes the want and violence experienced by prisoners of war, the philosophers of Paul's day used it metaphorically to describe a person without a right relationship to or proper understanding of God.[12] And, as we will see in chapter 7, ancient poets, philosophers, tragedians, and comedians portrayed similar wretched cries to depict a miserable creature desiring to do good but being impotent to do so.

Finally, in dejected lament, the *I*-figure squeaks, "Who will rescue me from the body of this death?" According to Craig Keener, since the wretch "does not even know the deliverer's name," the *I*-figure cannot be Paul, since the apostle clearly knows who will not only rescue him but will also make him more than a conqueror in Christ (8:37–39).[13] Immediately following this cry, then, Paul spills out the spoiler: *Thanks be to God through Jesus Christ our Lord!* (7:25). As mentioned above, some take this answer as evidence that the captive is a believer, while many scholars (like us) consider it an interjection, a

---

12. Thielman, *Romans*, 363.

13. Keener, *Mind*, 63. See also Moo, *Romans*, 271–72; and Robert Jewett, *Romans: A Commentary*, Hermeneia (Minneapolis: Fortress, 2007), 472.

taking off the mask as it were. The former group considers the desperate plea as something believers are waiting to experience, the latter regard it as the rescue believers already have in Christ Jesus, even if not yet completely received. About this, Bruce remarks: "Just how this deliverance from the power of indwelling sin may be appropriated is described more fully in the next chapter," but with this interjection, there is a glimpse of the realization that "the situation is not so hopeless as the 'wretched man' feared."[14]

After this thanksgiving, the *ego* concludes: "So then, on the one hand I myself with my mind am serving the law of God, but on the other, with my flesh the law of sin" (7:25 NASB). According to Frank Thielman, the conjunction, "so then," probably functions as it does elsewhere in Romans to signal "a summary of the foregoing discussion (8:12; 9:16, 18; 14:12, 19)."[15] Within this summary, Paul uses the emphatic *I* one last time, arguably to serve as a foil for a believer—the "I myself" alone standing in contradistinction to "those of us" in Christ alone. So, according to Stephen Chester, Paul makes a momentous switch here from the isolated *I* who lives under sin to those in Christ who walk together in the Spirit.[16] If so, this provides another blow against the Totally Paul position.

Delano Palmer adroitly captures Paul's line of reasoning in Romans 7.

> After affirming the fact that believers are dead to the law (vv. 1–6), and after launching a spirited defense in its behalf (vv. 7–11), Paul then employs a form of weakness language to further exculpate the law by pointing

---

14. Bruce, *Romans*, 158.

15. Thielman, *Romans*, 364.

16. Chester, "Retrospective View," 95.

out its inability to effect change in the "I" (vv. 14–17), enable the "I" to do good (vv. 18–20), and to emancipate the I" (vv. 21–24).[17]

Palmer goes on to argue that the absolute weakness of the wretch in chapter 7 sets up the promise of divine power for the believer in Romans 8.

4.1.4. ROMANS 8:1–2

Anyone trying to decipher the identity of the *ego* should not stop in 7:25, since the next two verses provide two more decisive clues.

> Therefore, there is *now* no condemnation for those who are in Christ Jesus, because through Christ Jesus the law of the Spirit who gives life has set *you/me* free from the law of sin and death. (8:1–2, author's translation, emphasis added)

First, Paul's use of the word "now" indicates that he transitions from the past unredeemed plight of the *I* to the present redeemed life of believers. In contrast to the miserable creature's situation in chapter 7, *now* liberation from the bondage of sin remains on offer. As Scot McKnight underscores, the reason believers escape condemnation is not merely because they are justified in Christ, but also because the Lord has liberated them from the law of sin and death.[18] As also mentioned above, this "now" demonstrates, to draw from Gordon Fee, that the Spirit

---

17. Delano Palmer, "Romans 7 Once Again: Intertextual Setting, Structure, and Rhetorical Strategy," *Caribbean Journal of Evangelical Theology* 16 (2017): 136. Palmer even drops a dad-joke here: "There is a sense in which Romans 6, 7, and 8 go together theologically (putting to rest the rumour that six was afraid of seven, because seven ate nine.)"

18. McKnight, *Romans*, 177.

is God's alternative to the law, his antidote to the flesh, and his solution to the wretch's plight.[19]

Another possible clue for decoding the identity of the I-figure is the singular pronoun Paul uses in 8:2: the law of the Spirit has set *you* [singular] free from the law of sin and death. He does not use the plural "you" here but the singular "you" that usually refers to an individual. Some consider the use of the singular as putting distance between the apostle and the *ego*.[20] If this is the case, it would be more like Paul saying to the Romans 7 man: "You, my miserable friend, have now been set free from the law of sin and death." But the apostle may use the singular here to address each individual reader "with this striking and joyful message of freedom."[21] Wright illustrates the gist by comparing it to "those old portraits whose eyes follow each onlooker around the room"; so also, he asserts, the declaration of freedom from sin "is aimed at every single hearer of the letter, whoever and wherever they may be."

To complicate the discussion further, some of our Greek texts do not have the singular pronoun "you" but the pronoun "me" instead.[22] In this case, the verse reads the law of the Spirit "has set *me* free from the law of sin and death." Whereas using the "you" possibly distinguishes Paul from the I in Romans 7, the "me" hints that the wretch in Romans 7 refers to Paul's *pre*-Christian life, which (as we will discuss in ch. 8) remains

---

19. Fee, *Empowering*, 515.

20. Stanley K. Stowers, *A Rereading of Romans: Justice, Jews, and Gentiles* (New Haven: Yale University Press, 1994), 281–82.

21. Wright, "Romans," 576. Cf. Witherington, *Romans*, 204.

22. E.g., Dirk Jongkind et al., eds., *The Tyndale House Greek New Testament* (Cambridge: Cambridge University Press, 2017). On the variant, see Bruce M. Metzger, *A Textual Commentary on the Greek New Testament*, 2nd ed. (New York: United Bible Societies, 1994), 456; and R. Dean Anderson, *Ancient Rhetorical Theory and Paul*, CBET 18 (Kampen: Kok Pharos, 1996), 178–83.

in our mind the most probable interpretation of the passage, regardless if the pronoun is "you" or "me."

4.2. CONCLUSION

Considering this paramount shift from Romans 7 to Romans 8, we can almost hear Paul declare, in direct contrast to the wretch's lament: "The things I want to do, I can now do, for the Lord has set me free, and he—not sin—lives in me!" While this is putting words in the apostle's mouth, in the next chapter we will look at Paul's words in his other letters. We will also see how what he says about other believers in those letters also collides with the words of the *I* in Romans 7.

5 ～

Here *Ego* Again

A Brief Exposition of Other Relevant Passages

Once on a layover in Amsterdam, I had the opportunity to see several of Rembrandt's paintings. While it is hard to pick a favorite, his *Self-portrait as the Apostle Paul* is up there. Faithful to the title, in the painting Rembrandt transposes his own face onto the apostle. The thought of it makes me chuckle, but it also reminds me of my own tendency to see myself in Paul rather than seeing Paul as himself.[1] As a result, I wrongly use his ancient words to make my contemporary points. Matthew Novenson calls this "hermeneutical ventriloquism" and warns that putting our words in the apostle's mouth can cause us to forget that his "words did not always mean what they eventually came to mean."[2]

---

1. For more on this, see Matthew V. Novenson, *Paul, Then and Now* (Grand Rapids: Eerdmans, 2022), 1.

2. Novenson, *Paul,* 3.

This is most likely what happened with the popular reading of Romans 7. We have sketched our own experience with sin onto Paul for so long that what we think the apostle says in Romans 7 is not what he meant to say in Romans 7. To redress this, we need to consider the apostle's other writings about how the Spirit enables Christians to say "NOPE" to sin, which in our mind deals one of the heaviest blows against the Totally Paul position. And perhaps the clincher is what the apostle explicitly says about himself outside of Romans 7. Having seen how the context of Romans 6–8 stands in opposition to the popular view, in this chapter, we will show how his comments elsewhere add to the case against it. First, we will investigate what Paul writes about himself in reference to sin and the law elsewhere and then what he says about believers with respect to them.

5.1. WHAT PAUL SAYS ABOUT HIMSELF ELSEWHERE

The four most relevant passages where Paul speaks autobiographically about sin and the law are Galatians 2; 1 Corinthians 15; Philippians 3; and 1 Timothy 1.

5.1.1. GALATIANS 2: CRUCIFIED WITH CHRIST

The first testimony we have from the apostle occurs in Galatians 2:11–21, where Paul recounts when he opposed Peter to his face for committing hypocrisy.

> But when Cephas came to Antioch, I opposed him to his face because he stood condemned. For he regularly ate with the Gentiles before certain men came from James. However, when they came, he withdrew and separated himself, because he feared those from the circumcision party. Then the rest of the Jews joined his hypocrisy,

so that even Barnabas was led astray by their hypocrisy. But when I saw that they were deviating from the truth of the gospel, I told Cephas in front of everyone, "If you, who are a Jew, live like a Gentile and not like a Jew, how can you compel Gentiles to live like Jews?" (Gal 2:11–14 CSB).

We would have loved to be there to see Paul tell Peter off and to hear Peter's response. We seriously doubt Peter, in turn, blurted something like: "Hey Paul, the things I want to do, I do not do. It's not me but sin living within me!"

Instead of going into detail regarding Peter's "deviation from the truth," Paul transitions to the concern of the men who caused Peter to stumble in the first place. These opponents likely feared that Paul's law-free gospel would promote Christ-followers to indulge their flesh because believers would wrongly conclude that they could continue in sin. The apostle responds to this assumption in a manner similar to Romans 6. It is God's grace not the law that energizes believers to live a righteous life. He also argues, to borrow from Erin Heim, that "Abraham's offspring are not those who take upon themselves the yoke of Torah, but rather those who receive their spiritual lineage through their adoption by God."[3]

To illustrate the ensuing liberty from this lineage, Paul places his new life in Christ over against his old one under the law.

For through the law I died to the law so that I might live for God. I have been crucified with Christ and *I no longer live, but Christ lives in me.* The life I now live in the body, I live by faith in the Son of God, who loved me and gave

---

3. Erin Heim, *Adoption in Galatians and Romans: Contemporary Metaphor Theories and the Pauline* Huiothesia *Metaphors,* BIS 153 (Leiden: Brill, 2017), 156.

> himself for me. I do not set aside the grace of God, for
> if righteousness could be gained through the law, Christ
> died for nothing! (Gal 2:19–21, emphasis added)

In brief, Paul follows Peter's failure by addressing his opponents' fear. He depicts his own life crucified with Christ, smothered in faith, and empowered by grace. Over against his opponents, he insists that the removal of the law does not lead to a life where the flesh is indulged but to the cross where it has been crucified.

Beverly Gaventa notes that Paul gives no sign that the death he experiences here is restricted to his dying to the law. Rather, she writes, "It is the whole of the *ego* that is gone." Gaventa states that while the apostle was of course "not asserting a non-bodily existence," she explains that "by moving to the language of 'life' and 'death' ... the register of the argument changes," so that "the canvas on which Paul portrays the gospel has enlarged from legal language to existential language." That is to say, the Lord does not simply justify a believer, he exists and dwells within her. According to Gaventa, the singularity of Paul's gospel involves an all-consuming character, with the radical result that "Now Christ is the one with whom 'I' am crucified, the one who lives 'in me.'"[4]

Paul's victorious proclamation here of "It is not I but Christ that lives within me" stands at odds with the wretch's defeated cry, "It is not I but sin that lives within me" (Rom 7:17). So also, the *ego*'s desperate resignation regarding being a slave to both God's law and to sin is quite unlike the apostle's confident "I died to the law" as well as his upbeat, autobiographical remark with which he concludes Galatians: "May I never boast except

---

4. Beverly Roberts Gaventa, "The Singularity of the Gospel Revisited," in *Galatians and Christian Theology: Justification, the Gospel, and Ethics in Paul's Letter*, ed. Mark W. Elliot et. al. (Grand Rapids: Baker Academic, 2014), 193–94.

in the cross of our Lord Jesus Christ, through which the world has been crucified to me, and I to the world" (Gal 6:14). Instead of being stretched between the two masters, sin and the law, Paul depicts a double crucifixion between him and the world. For the apostle, there is no "But I still serve sin with my body" stipulation here, nor any indication that he is a slave to anyone but Jesus Christ (Gal 1:10). Rather than on his incapacity to defeat sin, Paul defers to the conquest of the cross over his sin. Thereby, he stresses how he is done with sin, flesh, and the world—and how, by implication, we should be too.[5]

5.1.2. First Corinthians 15: I Yam What I Yam

The next relevant passage is 1 Corinthians 15, where Paul recites how the resurrected Christ appeared to the disciples. In 15:8–10, the apostle writes himself into the narrative:

> and last of all he appeared to me also, as to one abnormally born.
> For I am the least of the apostles and do not even deserve to be called an apostle, because I persecuted the church of God. But by the grace of God I am what I am, and his grace to me was not without effect. No, I worked harder than all of them—*yet not I, but the grace of God that was with me.* (Emphasis added)

Paul's self-denigrating comments about being "abnormally born" and "the least of the apostles" might at first ring of the fear and loathing in Romans 7. But, just as God's Spirit in Romans 8 eclipses the *ego*'s impotent defeat, so also God's grace here

---

5. See Joseph R. Dodson, "Paul and Seneca on the Cross: The Metaphor of Crucifixion in Galatians and *De Vita Beata,*" in *Paul and Seneca in Dialogue*, ed. Joseph R. Dodson and David E. Briones, Ancient Philosophy and Religion 2 (Leiden: Brill, 2017), 247–66.

transcends Paul's past deficits. In contrast to Popeye's famous line of moral resignation, "I yam what I yam and that's all that I yam," Paul proclaims that by the grace of God he is what he is and that makes all the difference. No longer constrained by his former life, divine grace now defines the apostle, outshining the sins that had rendered him unworthy. God's grace was so powerful and effective in Paul, it even gave him the vim and vigor that enabled him to work harder than even the legitimately born apostles. (Take that Peter and John!)

The apostle, of course, underscores that the credit for this good work goes only to God's grace working within him. So, as in Galatians, the apostle inserts another "not I, but x" equation. In comparison to the "not I, but Christ within me" construction from Galatians 2:19–21, in this passage Paul says, "not I, but God's grace that was with me." Once more, this contrasts starkly with the "not I, but x" equation in Romans 7:20 (cf. 2 Cor 4:10).

Galatians 2:20—**It is no longer I** ... *but* <u>Christ living in me</u>

1 Corinthians 15:10—**It is not I**, *but* <u>the grace of God with me</u>

Romans 7:20—**It is no longer I** ... *but* it is <u>sin living in me</u>.

While some consider sin as still dwelling in our bodies as an unwanted roommate alongside God's grace, his Spirit, and his Son, we are not certain Paul would consider this the case. Though sin's residue and stench remain, we suspect it got evicted at our baptism and now loiters at our door—begging, plotting, and pleading to get back in. Maybe in this way, sin is now akin to Bram Stoker's *Dracula*: unable to disturb our own private domicile, unless "we bid the monster in."[6] Either way, whether sin is in or out, these verses demonstrate that Christ *in* Paul and God's grace *with* Paul provide enough sway to help him live for God.

Paul goes on to assert that the Lord has proven him faithful as a servant of Christ. There is no mention here or elsewhere of being wracked with the frustration that characterizes the miserable creature in Romans 7. Conversely, what the apostle wrote earlier in 1 Corinthians stands at odds with the inner turmoil torturing the wretch. In 1 Corinthians 4:1–4, for instance, Paul boasts his conscience is clear—so much so that he is not aware of anything against him. The captive's claim to be under the law also grates against Paul's declaration in 1 Corinthians 9:20, "I myself am not under the law." It is difficult to square how Paul here, who is no longer under the law, could be the *I* in Romans 7, who, by his own confession, remains a slave to it.

5.1.3. Philippians 3: Pressing On

At the beginning of Philippians, Paul assures the church that whether he lives or dies, Christ will always be exalted in his body (Phil 1:20). Instead of bemoaning how sin dwelling within him prohibits him from doing good, he goes on to proclaim: "For to me to live is Christ and to die is gain. If I am to go on living in the body, this will mean fruitful labor for me" (1:21–22). Later when writing about this fruitful labor, Paul displays the same swagger he expresses in his other letters. For example, in Philippians 3, he sets himself over against the evildoers who place their mind on earthly things, who live to fill their

---

6. To extend the vampire metaphor, even if sin remains as an occupant, it'd be surrounded by a crucifix—which, as Van Helsing claims, causes the monster to calm down, lower his voice, and cautiously keep his distance. Cf. John Wesley, sermon 9, "The Spirit of Bondage and Adoption."

stomachs, and who boast in their shame (3:19). Whereas "these dogs and mutilators of the flesh" put their confidence in the flesh (3:2), Paul finds fortitude in the righteousness that comes from God, which is based on faith and not on the law (3:9).

Although some may want to limit this righteousness to a legal status, it is more probable that God's righteousness also gives Paul what he needs to grow in godliness. As Lynn Cohick writes, by righteousness from God, the apostle does not have in mind "today's assumption that being a Christian is all about holding a 'get out of jail free' card, and not thinking too much about God until you stand before the pearly gates with your card in hand." Instead, she says, it speaks "to the fullness of our salvation in Christ, which includes a lifelong deepening relationship."[7] The ramifications of this deepening relationship entail that, because of Christ's righteousness, we can live righteously. Paul has to qualify, though, that he still has work to do. Lest anyone think that he had achieved righteous perfection, he lets the church know he is not there yet.

> Not that I have already obtained all this, or have already arrived at my goal, but I press on to take hold of that for which Christ Jesus took hold of me. Brothers and sisters, I do not consider myself yet to have taken hold of it. But one thing I do: Forgetting what is behind and straining toward what is ahead, I press on toward the goal to win the prize for which God has called me heavenward in Christ Jesus. (Phil 3:12–14)

Again, in comparison to Romans 7, there is no trace here of an inability to make progress because of sin's possession of his

---

7. Lynn Cohick, *Philippians*, Story of God Commentary (Grand Rapids: Zondervan, 2013), 178.

body. Sure, Paul is not perfect and will not be until the return of Christ. But he gives no caveat expressing how even though he wants to run the good race he cannot because of his flesh. While Paul's constant portrayals of the pursuit of holiness as a race and a battle remind us that his victory over sin was by no means easy and automatic, we should be confident that victory did indeed come for Paul.[8] Even Romans 7, Bruce remarks, leads up to "a paean of triumph" for the apostle, after which "there is no further talk of defeat."[9]

Rather than frustration or any despair, the apostle exhibits in Philippians a resolved confidence similar to his proclamations in Galatians and 1 Corinthians. Paul advances assuredly toward his goal because Jesus has already achieved that goal for him. And he uses his success in progressing toward that righteousness to encourage believers to follow his example by also living up to what they have already attained (Phil 3:16–17).

Considering the wretch's failure to keep the law in Romans 7, we should also take into account Paul's certainty about his previous blamelessness with respect to the law.

> If someone else thinks they have reasons to put confidence in the flesh, I have more: circumcised on the eighth day, of the people of Israel, of the tribe of Benjamin, a Hebrew of Hebrews; in regard to the law, a Pharisee; as for zeal, persecuting the church; as for righteousness based on the law, *faultless*. (Phil 3:4–6, emphasis added)

Whereas the *I*-figure in Romans 7 struggles to fulfill the law, the apostle claims here that he observed it just fine. Many scholars

---

8. Bruce, *Romans*, 155.

9. Bruce, *Romans*, 162.

take Paul's "robust conscience" in this passage as a reason to rule out the apostle as the wretch in Romans 7, because, according to Paul's own words, his past life was free from the agony described by the miserable creature.[10] It would also seem bizarre for Paul to say he could fulfill the law before he met Christ but is powerless to do so now that he has the Holy Spirit.

5.1.4. *First Timothy 1: A Wretch Like Me*

Our last autobiographical example comes from 1 Timothy 1, where Paul discusses how the Lord considers him trustworthy, endues him with strength, and appoints him for service.

> I thank Christ Jesus our Lord, who has given me strength to do his work. He considered me trustworthy and appointed me to serve him, even though I used to blaspheme the name of Christ. In my insolence, I persecuted his people. But God had mercy on me because I did it in ignorance and unbelief. Oh, how generous and gracious our Lord was! He filled me with the faith and love that come from Christ Jesus.
>
> This is a trustworthy saying, and everyone should accept it: "Christ Jesus came into the world to save sinners"—and I am the worst of them all. But God had mercy on me so that Christ Jesus could use me as a prime example of his great patience with even the worst sinners. Then others will realize that they, too, can believe in him and receive eternal life. (1 Tim 1:12–16 NLT)

---

10. See Stendahl, "Paul," 199–215. Cf. A. Andrew Das, *Paul, the Law, and the Covenant* (Peabody, MA: Hendrickson, 2001), 215–33. According to Thielman, this probably describes how others viewed Paul more than revealing anything about his interior life (Thielman, *Romans*, 369).

Some might conclude that the apostle's comment regarding being the "worst of sinners" supports the Totally Paul interpretation. When we put this statement in context, however, we discover that the apostle considers himself the worst of sinners *not* based on a perpetual inability to do the good that he desires. Rather, he declares himself the worst of sinners because of his former life as a blasphemer, a persecutor, and a violent man. Paul's point is that if God saved him, the worst of sinners who fought against the church, God can save anyone.[11]

The apostle has also just juxtaposed himself as a righteous man over against wicked men who need the law. He remains God's faithful servant in contrast to Ephesus's wretched hive of villainy and scum. Over against these rapists, rebels, murderers, and slave traders, Paul boasts of a good conscience and a sincere faith. Once again the pathetic *ego* of Romans 7 does not comport with Paul's construal of himself as the example for how the Lord can take the worst of all sinners and make them trustworthy ambassadors of the gospel (1 Tim 1:8–11).

5.2. WHAT PAUL SAYS ABOUT BELIEVERS ELSEWHERE

Another colossal argument against the Totally Paul view is what the apostle writes about Christians everywhere else regarding their victory over sin. The highly attested popular view of Romans 7 represents the only place in Paul's letters (and the entire New Testament for that matter) stating or implying a believer is powerless to do any good because she is a captive to sin. But in contrast to the depiction of the wretch, plenty of passages give the impression that, with the power of Christ, the

---

11. Ben Witherington III, *A Socio-Rhetorical Commentary on Titus, 1–2 Timothy and 1–3 John* (Downers Grove, IL: InterVarsity Press, 2006), 199.

believer can overcome her flesh, since, rather than a life marked with misery and frustration, the Spirit produces in her joy and self-control. For the sake of brevity, we will give three examples: Romans 2, Galatians 5, and 1 Corinthians 10.

5.2.1. ROMANS 2: RIGHTEOUS GENTILES

While all the *I* in Romans 7 does is sin no matter what, some people in Romans actually do what the law requires and thereby demonstrate that it is written on their hearts.[12] For example, in Romans 2, Paul reasons:

> Indeed, when Gentiles, who do not have the law, do by nature things required by the law, they are a law for themselves, even though they do not have the law. They show that the requirements of the law are written on their hearts. (Rom 2:14–15)

Whereas scholars debate who these righteous gentiles are, the best interpretation concludes they are Christians like those in Romans 8 who, by the Spirit, fulfill the righteous requirement of the law.[13] In this case, Paul hints here of something he will expand upon later: namely that those who have been justified by Christ fulfill the law as they walk according to the Spirit (8:9). As mentioned above, these folks stand over against the wretch who is under the law and tethered to sin. Conversely, for the redeemed, the Lord has broken their chains and has written his law on their hearts. These law-fulfilling gentile believers in Romans 2 and 8 line up nicely with Paul's ministry goal stated

---

12. Paul may be speaking hypothetically here, but we do not think so.

13. Ambrosiaster, *Commentarius in Epistolam ad Romanos* 81.1.74–75; Jewett, *Romans*, 213; Simon J. Gathercole, "A Law unto Themselves: The Gentiles in Romans 2.14–15 Revisited," *JSNT* 24.85 (2002): 27–49.

at the start of the letter: namely, to call non-Jews to "the obedience that comes from faith" (1:5).

5.2.2. GALATIANS 5: ROBO-RIGHTEOUSNESS

Galatians 5:16–26 arguably stands out as the best passage for understanding the Christian struggle with sin. While some Totally Paul proponents point to 5:17 to support their view, the conflict in Galatians 5 is not identical to that in Romans 7. For one thing, in Romans 7:14–25, Paul never mentions the Spirit. Bruce rightly concludes, if the Spirit was in the mix, the portrayal in Romans 7 would be remarkably different and the result radically brighter.[14]

In Galatians, Paul does admit the flesh is alive and well, and he expounds on how its unholy appetites are contrary to the desires of the Spirit. But this tug-of-war between the Spirit and the flesh does not mean sin wins or even that the two powers eventually tie. This misreading is so strong, some English translations even freight this notion into the verse. For example, although the words "good intentions" are conspicuously absent from the Greek text, the New Living Translation reads:

> These two forces are constantly fighting each other, so you are not free to carry out *your good intentions*. (Gal 5:17, NLT emphasis added)

In contrast to the NLT, the New International Version provides a preferable rendering:

> They are in conflict with each other, so that you are not to do *whatever you want*. (Gal 5:17, emphasis added).

---

14. Bruce, *Romans*, 154.

The translators of the NIV seem to understand that Paul means the opposite of what the NLT expresses. The inability to carry out good intentions directly opposes what the apostle pens just before, "So I say, walk by the Spirit, and you will not gratify the desires of the flesh" (5:16 NIV). To underline how those who live in the Spirit *will not* fulfill the lusts of their flesh, Paul uses a construction that is the strongest way to negate something in Greek.[15]

In addition to that emphatic declaration, when looking at the literary context of the entire letter, we find that 5:16–17 is part of its recurring theme of how believers have freedom from both the law and sin, and how they must not use that liberty to satisfy their lusts. A fundamental piece of this thread can also be seen in 5:13, which sets up the purpose of the overall section in which 5:17 falls: "You, my brothers and sisters, were called to be free. But do not use your freedom to indulge the flesh" (author's translation). This promise of liberation here is also consonant with what Paul highlights at the beginning of Galatians: Christ gave himself to set believers free (1:4). The Christian liberty to reject sin becomes even clearer in light of what the immediate context of 5:17 espouses about the Spirit over the flesh.[16] Because of the crusade against the flesh, we are to walk by the *Spirit* (5:16), be led by the *Spirit* (5:18), and keep cadence with the *Spirit* (5:25). Believers live in the Spirit so that they do not obey the *flesh* (5:16), that they do not do

---

15. Namely, Paul uses the *ou mē* + aorist subjunctive here. For more on emphatic negation, see David Mathewson and Elodie Ballantine Emig, *Intermediate Greek Grammar: Syntax for Students of the New Testament* (Grand Rapids: Baker Academic, 2016), 168.

16. See John M. G. Barclay, *Obeying the Truth: Paul's Ethics in Galatians* (Minneapolis: Fortress, 1988).

whatever their *flesh* wants (5:17), and that they crucify the *flesh* along with its passions and desires (5:24).

In a nutshell, sin does not win the battle with God's Spirit. Believers are therefore branded, not with the deeds of the flesh, the fruit of which is obvious, but with the fruit of the Spirit, against which there is no law (5:23; 6:2, 17). To borrow from Novenson again, the Spirit of God allows believers, "or indeed compels them, to transcend the moral weakness of their corruptible bodies," yielding fruit of virtue within them.[17] Being driven by the Spirit to live a holy life means that walking by the Spirit consists, in the words of Christine Hays, of practicing "robo-righteousness," which, to expand on her thought, is like walking on a moving walkway instead of straining ahead under our own steam.[18]

5.2.3. FIRST CORINTHIANS 10: WAY OUT

In 1 Corinthians 10, Paul balances the promise of victory over sin with the real and present danger of falling back into it. As he warns in 10:12: "So, if you think you are standing firm, be careful that you don't fall!" But lest someone get the wrong idea that the sin against us is greater than the Spirit abiding within us, Paul does not stop there. In the next verse, he balances how Christ-followers can fall into temptation with how they can also escape it.

> No temptation has come upon you except what is common to humanity. But God is faithful; he will not allow you to be tempted beyond what you are able, but

---

17. Novenson, *Paul*, 3.

18. Christine Hays, *What's Divine about Divine Law? Early Perspectives* (Princeton: Princeton University Press, 2015), 48, 140–64.

with the temptation he will also provide the way out so
that you may be able to bear it. (1 Cor 10:13 CSB)

Since believers have a sure escape from temptation, they can
and should take it. As seen with the Corinthians, believers do
not always take "the way out" and as a result can become what
Paul refers to as fleshly and worldly. Yet, in this case, rather than
commiserating with the Corinthians, Paul scolds them for being
big babies who need to grow up and get along (1 Cor 3:1–3).
Unlike the miserable creature in Romans 7 whose body was
sold as a slave and controlled by sin, the Corinthian believers
were bought with a price—so that they are not their own and
therefore called to honor God with their bodies by no longer
allowing their desires to dominate them (1 Cor 6:18–20).

5.3. CONCLUSION

Considering what Paul writes in the passages above about his
life and the victory believers have over sin, the wretch's plight
stands out as peculiar. It makes me think of what I learned as
a child in the 1980s from Sesame Street's Cookie Monster who
would always sing about that one odd cookie on his tray: "one
of these is not like the others, one of these just does not belong."
The wretch, possessed by sin and unable to keep the law, fails
to correspond to the apostle inhabited by Christ, driven by
grace, and faultless concerning the law. From this chapter, we
see that the wretch is the odd cookie that is not like the others
and just doesn't belong.

The apostle does, of course, recognize a Christian's struggle with sin. In the contest, though, Paul expects the church to
resist the flesh and to exhibit victory over sin—not based on
our strength but on the truth that God has given us his Holy
Spirit (with a "robo-righteousness" that propels us), that he has

written his law on our hearts, and that he faithfully provides us a way out of temptation. Once more, against the constant and complete defeat by sin in Romans 7, Paul expresses everywhere else the expectation for believers to increasingly walk by the Spirit, and, to cite 2 Corinthians 7:1, to "purify ourselves from everything that contaminates body and spirit, perfecting holiness out of reverence for God."

6 ~

"But What About?"

Objections to the Not Paul View (Part 1)

Years ago I got to meet the honorable, the Most Reverend Bishop Hannah, the presiding bishop of the Methodist Church in The Gambia. In order to introduce her to our religion (I mean culture), we took her to a major league baseball game. At first, I thought I did a fair job explaining the rules to Bishop Hannah. But as the game progressed I had to keep qualifying aspects of the precious pastime I had taken for granted. Before too long, fans of both teams joined in to help me. "Yeah, a foulball is a strike except when ... right, he does usually play third, but sometimes infielders shift ... well, he can still run to firstbase after three strikes if ... no ma'am, that naked guy running on the field isn't (usually!) part of the game."

With Bishop Hannah, we saw our pastime again for the first time and realized how much of the inside of baseball we consider self-evident was altogether alien to our friend. When approaching challenging texts like Romans 7, we, like Bishop Hannah, step out of our world into another governed by its own rules, nuance, and particularity.[1] There are plays and players that were obvious to the first audience that make no sense to us. So, what may seem cumbersome to modern ears could be part and parcel of the culture of those to whom the letter was first directed. We believe most objections to the Not Paul view arise from a misunderstanding and unfamiliarity of the rhetorical game played in Rome. We hope we can do a better job explaining them to you than we did explaining baseball to Bishop Hannah.

There are eight big "but what abouts" used by Totally Paul interpreters to insist Romans 7 must refer to Paul's redeemed state:

1. But what about the intense tone?

2. But what about the thanksgiving in 7:25?

3. But what about the shift to present verb tenses in 7:14–25?

4. But what about an unbeliever desiring to do good and delighting in God's law?

5. But what about the phrase "inner-man"?

6. But what about the already-not-yet tension?

7. But what about my experience?

8. But what about the use of the *I*?

Due to the necessary density of each response, we have divided them into two chapters. Here we will address the first four objections and save the final four for the next chapter.

---

1. I am indebted to my student Nick Quinn for this line.

6.1. BUT WHAT ABOUT
THE USE OF THE *I*?

Some might argue the transition from using "we" in 7:6 to "I" in 7:7 means Paul is talking about himself as a believer.[2] Because of the surrounding context, however, many scholars consider the shift signifying that Paul is either impersonating someone else or talking about himself before his conversion.

Regarding the former, Richard Longenecker points out the distinction between what Greek geeks call the autobiographical *I* and the gnomic *I* which indicates people in general. For example, Paul uses the gnomic *I* in 1 Corinthians 13:1–3 to refer not specifically to himself but to anyone living without love.

> If I speak in the tongues of men or of angels, but do not have love, I am only a resounding gong or a clanging cymbal. If I have the gift of prophecy and can fathom all mysteries and all knowledge, and if I have a faith that can move mountains, but do not have love, I am nothing. If I give all I possess to the poor and give over my body to hardship that I may boast, but do not have love, I gain nothing. (1 Cor 13:1–3)

So also here in Romans 7, Longenecker asserts that Paul is using *I* to speak broadly of anyone living without God. He also adds that our English translations of *autos ego* as "I" or as "I myself" fail to bring out the intention of the Greek phrase, better rendered "I by means of my own resources and abilities, apart from God."[3]

---

2. E.g., C. E. B. Cranfield, *Romans: A Shorter Commentary* (Grand Rapids: Eerdmans, 1985), 159.

3. Longenecker, *Romans*, 636.

Stanley Stowers considers the "I myself" (*autos ego*) as even more than this. He argues that, with it, the apostle uses a "literary technique in which the speaker or writer produces speech that represents not himself or herself but another person or type of character."[4] According to Stowers, not only would Paul have been trained in school to employ this speech-in-character device but the audience would have been aware of it too. Stowers's conclusion has been widely accepted among scholars—to the point that it is arguably now the majority position.[5]

While we'd expect the apostle to write something like "okay, I'm going to do a speech-in-character now," according to Stowers, ancient readers and audiences would have been trained to look for or to hear a change of the voice alerting them that he was switching to another character.[6] Stowers asserts that Paul's introduction of the "You, O man" in Romans 2:1–16 would have first alerted the original audience that Paul was tuning up for the speech-in-character, and the abrupt change in 7:7 provided enough of a signal for them to recognize what the apostle was up to.[7]

If this seems too subtle for our contemporary ears, Stowers points out that this is how Origen, our earliest interpreter, read the passage.[8] The use of this rhetorical figure is also not as strange when one takes into account that Romans abounds with

---

4. Stowers, *Rereading*, 16–17.

5. It is not without its detractors; see Timmins, *Romans 7*, 12–34; and Will N. Timmins, "Romans 7 and the Resurrection of Lament in Christ: The Wretched 'I' and His Biblical Doppelgänger," *NovT* 61 (2019): 386–408.

6. Stowers, *Rereading*, 266–69.

7. Stanley K. Stowers, "Apostrophe, Προσωποποιία and Paul's Rhetorical Education," in *Early Christianity and Classical Culture: Comparative Studies in Honor of Abraham J. Malherbe*, ed. John Fitzgerald, Thomas Olbricht, and L. Michael White, NovTSup 110 (Leiden: Brill, 2003), 366–67. See also Dodd, *Paradigmatic*, 227–29; and McKnight, *Romans*, 174.

8. Stowers, *Rereading*, 264. Again, cf. Timmins, *Romans 7*, 12–34.

literary devices not often featured in his other letters (diatribe, litotes, sorites, personification, syllogism, and so on).[9] Another conspicuous clue for the audience regards how the miserable creature says he was alive and doing well *before* the coming of the law. The hearers would likely know that Paul was never "apart from the law." As a Jewish boy from the tribe of Benjamin, he was born under the covenant of Israel and circumcised on the eighth day (Phil 3:4–6).[10]

Although many scholars have been convinced by Stowers's argument, others respond with what we consider an even more likely proposal: Paul uses the *ego* because he is talking about himself *before his conversion* to show solidarity with his Jewish brothers and sisters and their collective history.[11] The pivot from past-Paul under the law to the present-Paul in the Spirit occurs with the "therefore now" in 8:1.[12] We will discuss this more in chapter 8.

---

9. As mentioned above, Stowers considers this as making sense of the singular "you" in 8:2, so that Paul responds to the wretch and delivers to him the news of freedom in Christ (Stowers, *Rereading*, 282).

10. That this refers to the period before Paul experienced puberty is unlikely. In a covenantal framework, a Jewish boy would not have ever been conveyed as "apart from the law"; see Chester, "Retrospective View," 72. See also Werner Georg Kümmel, *Römer 7 und das Bild des Menschen im Neuen Testament: Zwei Studien* (Munich: Kaiser, 1974), 75–84.

11. In this case the *ego* is both autobiographical (of Paul's past) as well as "representative" (of his nation).

12. As also mentioned above, the textual variant of 8:2, "has set *me* free," reinforces this view.

6.2. BUT WHAT ABOUT
THE INTENSE TONE?

Some argue that the tone of 7:14–25 is far "too realistic and vivid to be a purely rhetorical device," and that it is "impossibly theatrical if used of someone other than the speaker."[13] But this is exactly what ancient impersonation was designed to do. It is like modern method actors who do not simply represent their character. Rather, they become the character to provide an authentic portrayal of his or her emotions. We have similar figures in our literature. For instance, Flannery O'Conner explains that she depicts her characters hyperbolically so that her vision becomes "apparent by shock" to those who do not share her beliefs: "to the hard of hearing you shout, and for the almost-blind you draw large and startling figures."[14]

Along these lines, Gary Shogren argues that Paul takes on the role of an ancient satirist, known to use the first person in an intense tone to parody an opposing view. According to Shogren, the figure of the over-the-top wretch is what the apostle might have been expected to create if he were "being ironic, rejecting and recasting some established terminology and assumptions" such as the un-Pauline view that the law leads to liberty. Whereas O'Connor drew startling figures to depict the "Christ-haunted" South, Shogren considers the apostle's

---

13. Stott, *Romans*, 199; Morris, *Romans*, 296. See also J. Knox Chamblin, *Paul and the Self: Apostolic Teaching for Personal Wholeness* (Grand Rapids: Baker, 1993), 171; J. I. Packer, "The Wretched Man Revisited: Another Look at Romans 7:14–25," in *Romans and the People of God: Essays in Honor of Gordon D. Fee on the Occasion of His 65th Birthday*, ed. S. K. Soderlund and N. T. Wright (Grand Rapids: Eerdmans, 1999), 73–74; Johan Christiaan Beker, *The Triumph of God: The Essence of Paul's Thought* (Minneapolis: Fortress, 1990), 108.

14. Flannery O'Connor, "The Fiction Writer and His Country," in *Mystery and Manners: Occasional Prose*, ed. Sally Fitzgerald and Robert Fitzgerald (New York: Farrar, Straus & Giroux, 1969), 34.

move here as aimed at the law-centered synagogue, with the heightened emotions as part of the farce.[15]

In contrast to Shogren, Eastman considers the vividness not as Paul's way to parody his opponents but to relate pastorally to his audience. By the intonation, she maintains, the apostle assimilates "to the affective stance of the listener who experiences such bondage, thereby inviting him or her into a responsive identification with the speaker." The *I* thereby identifies with the audience and vice versa so that both the *ego* and the audience are extremely relieved when "together they hear Paul's words of affirmation" about how they are free at last from condemnation and sin.[16]

It could also be that Paul gives such a personal and emotional outpouring here because, in retrospect, he now understands the agony and what it was like for him before he met the Lord.[17] Again, we will discuss this option more in chapter 8.

6.3. BUT WHAT ABOUT THE THANKSGIVING IN 7:25?

As we have seen several times now, Paul follows the question "Who will rescue me from this body of death" with "Thanks be to God through Jesus Christ our Lord!" (7:25). This phrase is indeed a linchpin in the interpretation. If these are the words of the captive, it is difficult to deny that the wretch is a Christian. However, many scholars consider this as an example of an interjection.[18] Again, the first explanation for why this thanksgiving

---

15. Gary S. Shogren, "The 'Wretched Man' of Romans 7:14–25 as *Reductio ad absurdum*," *EQ* 72 (2000): 133.

16. Eastman, *Paul*, 116.

17. See Michael Winger, *By What Law? The Meaning of* Nomos *in the Letters of Paul*, SBLDS 128 (Atlanta: Scholars Press, 1992), 169.

18. Longenecker, *Romans*, 635.

in 7:25 represents Paul's voice and *not* that of the miserable creature goes as far back as the first extant interpretation of Romans 7, where Origen (a native Greek speaker) considered it an interjection. The thanksgiving regards Paul breaking character to remind the reader that the situation with the *I*-figure is no longer the case for the believer. As the apostle is about to clarify in Romans 8, God, through Christ and by the Spirit, has set the church free from the dominion of sin. Whereas we would prefer Paul to indicate this interjection with punctuation, in his day, there were no parenthetical markers.

It may also be helpful to notice that the last time Paul said "Thanks be to God!" was in Romans 6, where he reminds the readers that they are no longer slaves to the same sin that still controls the wretch. There, the apostle exclaims: "*But thanks be to God* that, though you used to be slaves to sin, you have come to obey from your heart the pattern of teaching that has now claimed your allegiance" (6:17, emphasis added).

In addition to understanding this phrase as an interjection, Thielman points out that it was typical for Paul either to begin or end a section of his argument "with themes that echo what has gone before or anticipate what comes next."[19] In this case, Paul inserts a foretaste of the freedom he'll expound upon in Romans 8. Witherington adds that in doing so, the apostle follows the technique Quintilian, the preeminent Roman rhetorician, attributed to skilled authors who overlap two subjects when moving from one topic to other for the sake of "force, energy, and pugnacity" (Quintilian, *Inst.* 9.4.129–30).[20] Witherington bemoans that the failure to understand this rhetorical play has led people to "the incorrect conclusion that Paul

---

19. E.g., 5:1–11; 7:13; Eph 2:5, 8–10. Thielman, *Romans*, 348.
20. Witherington, *Romans*, 196.

is speaking about Christians in 7:14–25." A mistake, he notes, "various early Greek Fathers who knew rhetoric did not make."[21]

Bruce Longenecker delineates how this common, elegant way of moving from one subject to another followed an A-b-a-B pattern. In this "chain-link transition," the big A represents a major discourse on a certain topic. Then, as the author prepares to transition from one subject to another, instead of an abrupt change, he or she provides a little b as a teaser for what is about to come. As part of the smooth transition, the author returns to the previous topic, but merely provides a brief comment to punctuate it, the little a. Finally, the writer is ready to go into the second main subject, the big B. According to Longenecker, in Romans 7–8, the chain-link transition looks like this:

A = Life under Law (7:9–24)

b = Life in Christ (7:25a)—"Thanks be to God through Jesus Christ" (CSB)

a = Life under Law (7:25b)—"With my mind I myself am serving the law of God" (CSB)

B = Life in Christ (8:1–12)

So, for the the sake of force and flow, Paul inserts an interjection (b), which alerts the reader that he is about to move from the topic of life under the law (A, a) to the next topic about life in Christ (B).[22]

---

21. Witherington, *Romans*, 196.

22. Bruce W. Longenecker, *Rhetoric at the Boundaries: The Art and Theology of the New Testament Chain-Link Transitions* (Waco, TX: Baylor University Press, 2005), 92.

6.4. BUT WHAT ABOUT THE SHIFT
TO PRESENT TENSE VERBS?

We have saved this objection for the last one in this chapter because it gets deep into the Greek grammatical weeds. (One might say it even gets *tense*.) We would avoid it altogether if we could, but this argument has been used to claim Paul is talking about himself as a believer in 7:14–25. The reasoning goes something like this: since Paul shifts from the past tense to the present tense, he must be talking about his current Christian experience.[23]

To begin, Paul does not actually use past or present tense verbs. Rather, what some people refer to as past tense verbs are what scholars call aorist-tense verbs. Aorist does not mean past time. It is instead an undefined tense—bland, ambiguous, and vague. So also, the present tense, despite the name given to it, does not necessarily imply present time, if at all.[24]

Whereas scholars debate the exact nuance of the aorist and present tenses, hardly any consider the aorist as equivalent to our English past tense, or the present tense the same as our present tense.[25] More than present time, for instance, the present tense verbs are used for some type of emphasis. In this case, to borrow from Jae Hyun Lee, the tense change probably provides "a more vivid effect to the miserable situation of humans who are under the power of sin" because they are still living under the weakness of the law.[26] If anyone argues for a Totally

---

23. E.g., de Waal Dryden, "Revisiting Romans 7," 129–51.

24. See Mathewson and Emig, *Intermediate Greek*, 119–33.

25. This concept is called "verbal aspect." It gets confusing. Mike Aubrey has the best explanation out there for non-Greek students, https://koine-greek.com/2021/12/15/a-brief-guide-to-aspect-in-greek-part-i/.

26. Jae Hyun Lee, *Paul's Gospel in Romans: A Discourse Analysis of Rom 1:16–8:39*, Linguistic Biblical Studies 3 (Leiden: Brill, 2010), 380. See also Kruse, *Romans*, 305; and Keener, *Mind*, 63–65. Cf. Timmins, *Romans 7*, 156.

Paul view based on a pivot from past to present tense, he or she may be working from outdated scholarship.[27] As Schreiner puts it: "the use of the present tense is hardly a decisive argument" here.[28] While there is a significance with the change, the shift indicates that Paul is using the verb to turn up the volume, not to identify the captive as a Christian, but to stress his condition as an unbeliever.

The biggest pivot from past to present time is not found in the verb tenses in 7:14–25 but in the emphatic now of 8:1, which underscores how what was the situation for believers in Romans 7, before they met Christ, should no longer be the case for them.[29]

6.5. CONCLUSION

In this chapter, we have done our best to address the most common arguments regarding why Paul must be talking about the Christian life in Romans 7. First, just because Paul uses *I* does not mean he is talking about himself in the present. It could be a gnomic *I*, a speech-in-character, or a reference to his life before Christ. Next, his intensity does not mean he himself is experiencing this defeat to sin. Instead, the tone could reflect his past frustration, or a rhetorical feature specifically designed to be vivid for the sake of parody or pastoral persuasion. Third, on closer inspection, Paul's "But thanks be to God!" in 7:25 follows his use of a parenthetical interjection in his letters as well as a common way to transition to a new topic. In support of this interpretation, the first interpreter of Romans 7 did not

---

27. Will Timmins commented, "Very few present-day scholars argue for some form of post-conversion reading of ego on the basis that the present tense *grammaticalizes* time" (by email, Sept. 4, 2022).

28. Schreiner, *Romans*, 379.

29. Longenecker, *Romans*, 649.

take this thanksgiving as coming from the mouth of the wretch either. Finally, according to Greek scholars, the shift to present tense verbs does not prove that Paul is speaking in present time but instead that he is somehow magnifying, highlighting, and accentuating the desperate experience of the wretch.

7 ∼

"But What About?"

Objections to the Not Paul View (Part 2)

One day I was hiking on the Oregon coast with my eighteen-month-old granddaughter on my back. As we were climbing to the summit that looked out upon the mighty Pacific gloriously punctuated with the likes of Haystack Rock, I playfully said to her, "Midge, you're getting heavy." She retorted: "Not heavy, Pop, I'm happy!" To my delight, she didn't want to stop. As we have taken you halfway through some heavy responses to common rebuttals from the Totally Paul proponents, we hope you too are happily ready for more. In this chapter we will cover the last four of their objections—related to how the wretch delights in the law, how he refers to his inner man, how he fits in the already-not-yet tension, and how many believers identify with his tragic experience.

7.1. BUT WHAT ABOUT AN UNBELIEVER DESIRING TO DO GOOD AND DELIGHTING IN GOD'S LAW?

Not only do we often miss things in the text that the original audience would have assumed, but we also bring to it our own presuppositions and theological baggage. For example, due to the deeply ingrained doctrine of total depravity, many Protestants may not have a box for an unbeliever desiring to do good and delighting in God's law. If this is true, the wretch must be a Christian since the *I* seeks good and aligns itself with the law.[1] Yet again, what may be foreign to us may have been familiar in the early church.

For instance, Origen argues that Paul demonstrates how "even the man who is carnal and sold under sin may try to resist evil."[2] And, as we saw in chapter 2, John Calvin also acknowledges that nonbelievers have uttered similar sentiments (even though he says they don't count). In this first part of this section, we will look at some of these confessions from unbelievers in secular literature. Then we will investigate the parallels from non-Christian Jewish authors who love the law and abhor sin. We hope these two categories will put to bed the notion that only believers desire to do good and delight in the law.

7.1.1. UNBELIEVING GENTILES

There are various places in ancient non-Christian works that instantiate how pagans strongly desired to do good but were unable to do so. Examples can be found in Latin poetry and Roman philosophy.

---

1. Garland, *Romans*, 246.
2. Origen, *Comm. Rom.* 3.272.

7.1.1.1. Latin Poetry

For instance, the widely popular first century poem "Medea" contains comments resonating with those of the miserable creature. As we will see below, the story became an accepted source to depict a person's inner war that results from her knowing what is right versus her crushing desire to do otherwise.[3] In the poem, Ovid gives voice to Medea's agony as she fights the overpowering passion within her.[4] Not being able to calm the torturous desires in her mind, she cries aloud to herself: "In vain, Medea, do you fight." In talking to herself, she comes to discover the real reason her battle is futile: she had been infiltrated by a force that bewitched her senses and chained her will.

Realizing she is being ruled by this invincible power, she blurts in desperation: "You poor, unlucky soul!" (*Metam.* 7.16, author translation).[5] (In another version, she laments: "What have I done wretched woman? Wretched woman?" [Seneca, *Medea* 989–990]). Frustrated, Ovid's Medea continues: "Ah, if I could, I should be more myself. But some strange power drags me on against my will. Desire persuades me one way, reason another." Crestfallen, she concludes, "I see the better and approve it, but I follow the worse" (*Metam.* 7.20–21 [LCL]).

Considering this poem's poignancy, it comes as no surprise that Medea grew to be a classic example in the first century to define what it means to be wretched, serving as the case in point for when a person says:[6]

---

3. Thielman, *Romans,* 357.

4. Ovid, *Metam.* 7. Much of the setting for "Medea" takes place in Corinth, where Paul writes Rom 7 from.

5. Cf. Horace Gregory, trans., *Ovid: The Metamorphosis* (London: Penguin, 1958).

6. Cf. Max J. Lee, *Moral Transformation in Greco-Roman Philosophy of Mind: Mapping the Moral Milieu of the Apostle Paul and His Diaspora Jewish Contemporaries,* WUNT 2/515 (Tübingen: Mohr Siebeck, 2020), 287–88.

I want something, and it does not happen; and what
creature is more wretched than I? I do not want something, and it does happen; and what creature is more
wretched than I? (Epictetus, *Disc.* 2.17, 19–20 [LCL])

Not only is Medea's psychological struggle relevant to the agony
of the miserable creature in Romans 7, but her self-awareness
amid it also parallels his. In other words, like the *I*-figure,
Medea isn't blinded by her passion. She comprehends that it
is compelling her. Even though she calls her urge an unknown
power, ironically, she knows enough to identify it. Also, despite
her overwhelming lust, she (like the *ego*) still knows the right
thing to do.

It is beyond the scope of this book to discuss whether Paul
or the audience would have noticed parallels between Medea
and the *I* in Romans 7. We simply submit it as one example
of a widespread secular work describing an unbeliever who
wanted to do good but could not because she realized she was
captive to a vicious power.

7.1.1.2. *Greco-Roman Philosophy*

Our next examples come from two philosophers who wrote
in the capitol around the same time Paul penned Romans:
Seneca and Epictetus. In his writings, Seneca bewails how "no
one has knowledge of God" or holds him in reverent esteem.
Rather, people "sink themselves in pleasures" until they cannot
do without them, until they serve their desires more than they
enjoy them. According to the philosopher, humanity grasps
after vice until they find themselves in vice's grip, fettered to
its lusts. Having wallowed in sin for so long, the masses are
not merely defiled by fleshly desires. They are deeply dyed by
them. Seneca considers himself no exception to this rule. Along

with everyone else, his spiritual malady is not that of a sore on his foot but of an abscess deep within his chest (*Ep.* 31.10; 39.6; 59.9; 68.8).

Yet Seneca elucidates that despite his moral gout, he still longs for virtue, seeks after salvation, and stretches for the light. With all his might, he strives to be liberated from sin and released from its cross, struggling day-by-day to wrestle his body away from its beams (*Vit. beat.* 18–20; *Ep.* 6.1, 59.9–10; 71.36–37; 75.16; 87.4–5). He informs his reader that he will rail against his sins in the hopes that the time will come when he will live as he ought because he will finally be able to live as he ought. Nevertheless, he confesses, he will never stand upright unless he is stirred by god's spirit and propped up by the divine (*Ep.* 41.5; 73.16).

Epictetus's teaching about a person's internal conflict also has parallels to Romans 7. He writes: "For since the one sinning does not desire to sin but to walk uprightly, it is clear that he indeed does *not* do what he desires" (*Disc.* 2.26.1, emphasis added). According to the philosopher, as long as the man doesn't realize he is failing to do the good he desires, he is living a lie (*Disc.* 2.26.3). Epictetus comments that others share in the blame when they fail to point out to him that "he is not doing what he wishes, but is doing what he does not wish to do instead" (*Disc.* 2.26.4–6). In this vein, Epictetus rebukes sinners who walk according to the flesh and cry out "For what am I? A miserable, paltry man!" He also responds frankly to those who lament, "Lo, my wretched, paltry flesh." They are wretched indeed, he agrees. Therefore he instructs them to directly leave their degraded desires and to cleave instead to the transformative truth that they are begotten of God (*Disc.* 1.4.1–6).

These examples demonstrate that the first-century world contained unbelievers who desired to do good but did not do the good they desired. These instances from both epic poetry and Roman philosophy also manifest how the plight of the wretch in Romans 7 has popular parallels contemporaneous with Paul's letter. Despite these relevant examples from pagan authors, as we will see in the next section, the wretch's monologue resonates even more with the longings and struggles of those in the Hebrew Bible who loved the law but failed to keep it.

7.1.2. OLD TESTAMENT ISRAEL AND PAUL'S UNBELIEVING KINSFOLK

7.1.2.1. Old Testament Israel

Two immediate thoughts spring to mind with respect to the Israelites and the Torah, their law. The first regards Israel's songs about their love of, zeal for, and commitment to it. The gushing over the law's statues, commandments, and decrees in Psalm 119 is especially consonant with how the *I* in Romans 7 serves the law and delights in it. For example, the psalmist proclaims how his soul is steadily consumed with longing for God's marvelous laws. He pants and pines for the perfect, everlasting law, which is right and true, more precious to him than costly jewels (Ps 119:20, 70–72, 97, 127–160). Enraptured, he interjects "Oh, how I love your law! I meditate on it all day long!" (119:174).

This leads to the second idea that comes to mind with respect to the Israelites and the Torah: namely, the accounts of their failure to keep the law threaded throughout the Hebrew Bible.[7] This thread also appears in Psalm 119, where he wails because his people do not obey the law, and he prays no sin

---

7. Cf. Beverly Roberts Gaventa, "The Shape of the 'I': The Psalter, the Gospel, and the Speaker in Romans 7," in *Apocalyptic Paul: Cosmos and Anthropos in Romans 5–8*, ed. Beverly Roberts Gaventa (Waco, TX: Baylor University Press, 2013), 77–92.

will rule over him causing him to break it too (119:133–136). Nevertheless, despite his detest for sin, he is compelled to groan in self-condemnation: "If only my ways were committed to keeping your statutes! Then I would not be ashamed when I think about your commands" (119:5–7 CSB). The psalmist goes on to liken himself to a "wineskin in the smoke," shrunk and shriveled, with eyes weary from looking for the Lord. Whereas at times he expresses confidence that he keeps the law, the last note of the song belies his certainty. "I have strayed like a lost sheep" (119:176).

Considering their mutual preoccupation with the law and their shared state of affliction, one might conclude the wretch in Romans 7 has a twin, a Doppelgänger, in the Psalms.[8] Either way, Psalm 119 captures how law-loving Israelites deplored sin and delighted in Torah, even as they cried out in shame because they had strayed away. As a result, they lament because, regardless of their desires to uphold the law, they did not observe its ways.

7.1.2.2. Paul's Unbelieving Kinfolk

What Paul writes in Romans about his unbelieving Jewish brothers and sisters echoes the psalmist's love for the law and his people's inability to fulfill its righteous requirements. His current kinfolk also zealously pursued the righteousness of the law but failed to submit to it (see Rom 9:31). Accordingly, in Romans 10:5–8, Paul plays with Moses's words about how despite the commands not being too difficult to achieve, the Hebrews would still fail to follow them (Deut 30:11–18). After Moses made this pronouncement, the Lord affirms that Israel will indeed constantly break the covenant. To stress the point,

---

8. See Timmins, "Lament in Christ," 386–408.

God gives Moses a song to teach the people. This song is going to be stuck inside their heads, as it testifies against them from their own mouths how they'd continue to break the law of the Lord (Deut 31–32).

For Paul, his unbelieving kindred are still living like this and reflect what the rest of the Hebrew Bible bears out regarding how God's people fail to keep his law, which results in their exile (see Ps. 106:34–43). As Scripture shows, even when the Lord brought the chosen people back from captivity, they continued to flounder. For instance, Malachi proclaims to postexilic Israel that God longs to shut the door of his temple because they have broken his covenant and profaned his name. The Lord is so angry with them for not keeping the law, he desires to take the sacrificial waste and spread it on their face (Mal 1–2). Nonetheless, he tells Malachi another, less messy, plan. In the last days, God will send the prophet Elijah to prepare the way for the coming of the Lord. According to Paul, God has fulfilled this promise in Jesus Christ so that now believing Israel can do what unbelieving Israel could not.[9]

In brief, the wretch in Romans 7, who delights in the law despite an inability to keep it, looks more like the depiction of Paul's people who struggled to obey the law than what the apostle says about believers in his letters. As we will see in the next chapter, these parallels from the Hebrew Bible comport especially well with the interpretation of the *ego* as unredeemed Israel.

---

9. Cf. Brant Pitre, Michael P. Barber, and John A. Kincaid, *Paul: A New Covenant Jew; Rethinking Pauline Theology* (Grand Rapids: Eerdmans, 2019), 48.

7.2. BUT WHAT ABOUT THE
PHRASE "INNER MAN"?

It may be argued that Paul's reference to the inner man in 7:22 reveals that the wretch is a believer. The other time the apostle uses the term it refers to Christians (2 Cor 4:16). Of course the mention of a believer having an inner self does not rule out an unbeliever having one too. In fact, for many in the Roman world, the term *inner person* would remind them of the frequent discussion about the contest between reason and desire wherein the soul attempts to tame and suppress the flesh (Plato, *Resp.* 589a).

Wasserman demonstrates how well Romans 7 fits into this philosophical tradition that was engaged in depicting "the radical disempowerment of reason at the hands of the passions."[10] Wasserman notes that while the portrayal of inner turmoil in desiring to do good but being powerless to do so rarely occurs in Paul's letters, the theme was a popular conversation in his day. She also exhibits how these discussions often contained metaphors and other stock terms that recur in Romans 7. Terms such as "inner person," "mind," "beautiful," and "good" peppered the pages of these secular writings about moral progression. Paul's depiction of sin in Romans 7 also parallels the philosophers' construal of passion as an "indwelling being that makes war, enslaves, imprisons, and sometimes even metaphorically kills the mind."[11]

Along these lines, Joshua Jipp argues that the wretch's speech in Romans 7 echoes Plato's description of the inner man in the *Republic*.[12] There, Plato has Socrates discuss the phenomenon

---

10. Wasserman, "Death," 800.

11. Wasserman, "Death," 794.

12. Jipp, "Educating," 231.

referred to as *akrasia*, the internal struggle wherein a person chooses to go against their better judgment because of their lack of willpower. Socrates illustrates this phenomenon with a man named Leontius. As the story goes, once when Leontius was walking by some executed criminals, there suddenly arose in him the dual desire both to look upon the bodies of the victims and to veil his eyes from the hideous sight. Although he did not want to surrender to his base appetites, he could not help it and yielded to the temptation. Angry at his lack of self-control, he bolted towards the corpses, forced his eyes wide open, and yelled to his eyeballs: "There, O evil wretches, look all you want and take your fill. Are you happy now?!" (*Resp.* 440a, author paraphrase).

Socrates goes on to use another example: a fool who thinks he is free because he can do what he wants, when he wants, and how he wants. In reality though, this man is enslaved because he chooses to indulge his appetite rather than to listen to reason. His pursuit of pleasure results in his soul's misery since he does the opposite of what his inner man really wants. Yet because his soul is "driven and drawn by the gadfly of desire," his inner man is full of frustration and repentance (*Resp.* 577d [LCL]). According to Socrates, because the soul longs to obey reason, any person in bondage to worldly pleasure will eventually erupt into an anguished crescendo of lamentations, wailings, and groans (like the wretch does in Romans 7).[13]

---

13. Jipp, "Educating," 248.

7.3. BUT WHAT ABOUT THE
"ALREADY-NOT-YET" TENSION?

"The depth of defeat and captivity to sin" that the *ego* experiences stands as the most significant objection to the Totally Paul view.[14] Of this, Williams states that sin rules over the believer "is nonsensical in light of Paul's argument in Romans 6 that the believers have died to sin and that the power of sin no longer reigns over them."[15] Most proponents of the popular view try to get around the contradiction by appealing to the already-not-yet tension that marks Paul's theology.[16] For example, according to Marvin Pate, the admixture of Christian liberation and bondage is "the result of the overlapping of the two ages."[17] So, in this case, as Schreiner puts it, "believers have already been liberated from the dominion of sin, but in the already-not-yet situation *there is still bondage to sin until the day we die*."[18] In short, for them, it's complicated. We are slaves to sin, but we're not, but kind of.

While the already-not-yet tension is valid for Paul's letters in general, the apostle frames the wretch's monologue with a "back-then-but-now" paradigm. *Back then* we were in the flesh (7:5), *but now* we serve in the new way of the Spirit 7:6). *Back then* we were in bondage to the law of sin (7:14–25), *but now* the law of the Spirit has set us free (8:1–2). This model also works better in 6:21–22. There, Paul asks the believers what benefit they reaped *back then* when they did the things they are now ashamed of, which result in death (6:21). "*But now* that you have

---

14. Schreiner, *Romans*, 385.

15. Williams, *One New Man*, 50.

16. E.g., de Waal Dryden, "Revisiting Romans 7," 129–51. Cf. Witherington, *Romans*, 204.

17. Marvin Pate, *Romans*, Teach the Text (Grand Rapids: Baker, 2013), 176.

18. Schreiner, *Romans*, 385 (emphasis added).

been set free from sin and have become slaves of God, the bene-fit you reap leads to holiness, and the result is eternal life" (6:22) This is also the case for 8:9 where Paul comments how *back then* believers were in the realm of the flesh, *but now* they are in the domain of the Spirit since the Spirit of God dwells within them. So, unless Paul subtly slides into the already-not-yet tension in 7:14–25, the expectation seems to be *back then* believers under the law were living in the flesh, serving sin, and bearing fruit for death (Rom 7), *but now* they should be living in the Spirit, walk-ing in new life, and bearing fruit for God (Rom 8).

7.4. BUT WHAT ABOUT
MY EXPERIENCE?

This final question relates to the popular parable about a man who taps on an aquarium to ask a goldfish: "How's the water in there?" In response, the fish darts away and reports to another fish what happened. "Did you hear that guy? He asked me how the water was. What's water?" Hence the axiom goes: If you want to know what water is, don't ask the fish. For many of us, we have been swimming in dirty tanks for so long, we can barely imagine life outside of our bowl. We reason Romans 7 must be the experience of Paul as a Christian because it's our experience as Christians. "How can we doubt that this is true for Paul when it is so true for us?"[19]

But one of the first rules of Bible interpretation is to avoid reading our own baggage into a text. As Stott writes: "It is never wise to bring to a passage of Scripture our own ready-made agenda, insisting that it answers our questions and addresses our concerns. For that is to dictate Scripture instead of listening

---

19. John Knox, *Life in Christ Jesus: Reflections on Romans 5–8* (New York: Seabury, 1961), 67.

to it." According to Stott, instead "we have to lay aside our pre-suppositions, so that we can conscientiously think ourselves back into the historical and cultural setting of the text." Then we shall be, Stott concludes, "in a better position to let the author say what he does say and not force him to say what we want him to say."[20] So, since context determines meaning, (borrowing again from Anaïs Nin) we want to try to see the *I* through Paul's first-century Jewish eyes not from our modern perspective.

It too may be inaccurate to say utter defeat by sin is the experience of *every* believer. Not only is it difficult to find this presupposition anywhere else in the New Testament, but, even if it is the case for most believers, it does not also follow that it *must* be. We agree with Leon Morris that more often than not the believer is to be on top, victorious over sin, and at peace with God.[21]

Ironically, most of our friends who hold the popular view of Romans 7 firmly preach against interpreting the Bible based on experience, except it seems for this passage. With that said, we admit again that we too struggle with sinful, selfish, and sultry desires. Thus, we are not making light of the ongoing war believers have with the flesh. Rather, while validating our campaign against sin as real and painful, we believe that, with Romans 8, Paul taps on the glass to let us know we can increasingly swim in clearer water. We will talk about this more at the end of the book.

---

20. Stott, *Romans*, 189.

21. Morris, *Romans*, 288. Cf. J. C. Ryle, *Holiness: Its Nature, Hindrances, Difficulties, and Roots* (Carlisle: Banner of Truth, 2014), 101.

7.5. CONCLUSION

We have now responded to four more common objections from the Totally Paul view. First, although some may struggle to envision a non-Christian who desires to do good or who delights in God's law, we have shown numerous examples from unbelieving gentiles and Jewish people alike that harmonize with the words of the *I* in Romans 7. Next, we elucidated how the wretch's use of *inner man* was common in Greek philosophy for a pagan desiring to do good but being defeated by a resident evil power instead. Third, we argued that reading the already-not-yet tension into Romans 7 does not fit as well as the back-then-but-now paradigm that frames the wretch's lament. Finally, we remarked that we should not interpret Romans 7 based on our experience but on the rules of proper interpretation. If the *ego*'s plight of constant and complete defeat by sin is still our experience, Romans 6 and 8 tells us that it does not have to be anymore.

8 ∼

The *I*'s Have It

Alternative Identities for the Ego

After we had moved to Colorado, my mother-in-law sent us a text about finding an Airbnb near us that allowed dogs. Her next text said, "Well, the advertisement says 'pot-friendly,' but I think they meant 'pet-friendly.'" We were glad the conversation was over text so that she could not see us spew our coffee out when we read her Southern Baptist interpretation of the ad. We delicately informed her that since the Airbnb was in Denver, we were pretty sure it wasn't a typo. So also, considering the original context of Romans 7, we remain confident that Paul did not intend to describe a typical Christian utterly defeated by sin. But if not, who then is the wretch behind the mask? Below, we will give seven possible answers: (1) Adam and Eve, (2) Israel, (3) past-Paul; (4) an almost Christian; (5) the interlocutor; (6) anyone under the law; (7) it's more complicated than that. We will take these options one by one, starting with the first human couple. Even though we mainly land on the "past-Paul" option, we acknowledge the validity of the others, more or less.

8.1. ADAM, EVE, AND *EGO*

Some scholars see Paul not writing an autobiography of himself as much as a biography of the first man, with sin corresponding to the snake in the garden.[1] These scholars argue the *I* has a name, and it is Adam.[2] For one thing, as Brian Dodd mentions, Romans 7 follows the same sequence as Genesis 3: innocence → command → transgression → death.[3] According to Morna Hooker, Paul has both alluded to and explicitly drawn on Genesis 1–3 from the beginning of the letter.[4] Of course, the apostle had also just spent an entire section in Romans 5 discussing Adam in association with sin, law, and death. And the parallels between 5:12–21 and 7:8–13 are particularly apparent.

As we have seen, Paul places the first Adam in stark contrast to the Second Adam, Jesus Christ, whose obedience brought righteousness, grace, and life. While the former existence in the old Adam parallels the wretch in 7:9–25, life in the Second Adam harmonizes with 8:1–17.

---

1. Matthew Black, *Romans*, NCB (Grand Rapids, Eerdmans, 1984), 102.

2. E.g., Christian Grappe, "Qui me délivrera de ce corps de mort? L'esprit de vie! Romains 7,24 et 8,2 comme éléments de typologie adamique," *Bib* 83 (2002): 472–92. I am indebted here to Hermann Lichtenberger, my supervisor at the University of Tübingen; see his *Das Ich Adams und das Ich der Menschheit: Studien zum Menschenbild in Römer 7*, WUNT 164 (Tübingen: Mohr Siebeck, 2004), 1–328.

3. Dodd, *Paradigmatic*, 225.

4. E.g., Morna D. Hooker, "Adam in Romans 1" *NTS* 6 (1960): 297–306. Cf. Derek R. Brown, "'The God of Peace Will Shortly Crush Satan Under Your Feet': Paul's Eschatological Reminder in Romans 16:20a," *Neot* 44 (2010): 1–14.

Adam, Sin, Death and the Law in 5:12–21 (CSB)	The *Ego*, Sin, Death and the Law in 7:8–13 (CSB)
Sin entered the world through one man, and death through sin, in this way death spread to all people.	Once I was alive apart from the law, but when the commandment came, sin sprang to life and I died.
Sin was in the world before the law, but sin is not charged to a person's account when there is no law.	Sin, seizing an opportunity through the commandment, produced coveting in me. For apart from the law sin is dead.
Death reigned from Adam to Moses ... by the one man's trespass the many died.	The commandment ... resulted in death for me. For sin ... deceived me, and through it killed me.
By the one man's trespass, death reigned through that one man.... The law came along to multiply the trespass.	Sin ... was producing death in me ... so that through the commandment, sin might become sinful beyond measure.

This Adam interpretation reminds us that, rather than reading Romans piecemeal (a little here, a little there), the original audience listened to the letter sequentially. Since they already had the first man on their minds when they came to Romans 7, an impersonation of him here would not have been a stretch for them. But even if the readers had so quickly forgotten Romans 5,

Paul still hides Edenic clues in plain sight (some low-hanging fruit, so to speak).

First, for Paul, only one man was ever "alive apart from the law"—Adam. This led to the famous dictum by Käsemann: "There is nothing in the passage which does not fit Adam, and everything fits Adam alone."[5] Through Adam, sin entered the world and brought death. But what about the law in Genesis 3? Well, not only is the same Adamic sin-death pattern displayed with the wretch, but Jewish exegesis also viewed the command not to eat of the tree of the knowledge of good and evil as Adam's receiving the whole Torah in a nutshell. Even more relevant, the first man's disobedience of that prohibition was considered a breach of the "Do not covet" commandment—the very prohibition Paul had just quoted in 7:7.[6]

Second, the whole "sin deceived me, and I died" line smacks of the fall and the damming result of the serpent's lie. Notice the parallel:

Romans 7:11: "sin deceived me [*ex*ēpatēsen me*] and I died." (author's translation)

Genesis 3:13: "the snake deceived me [*ēpatēsen me*] and I ate." (author's translation)

With the mention of deception, other scholars think we got the wrong *man*. Rather than our father Adam, they believe Paul is impersonating our mother Eve.[7] Nicholas Elder, for exam-

---

5. Käsemann, *Romans, 196.*

6. See A. J. M. Wedderburn, "Adam in Paul's Letter to the Romans," in *Studia Biblica 1978, 3: Papers on Paul and Other New Testament Authors*, ed. E. A. Livingstone, JSNTSup 3 (Sheffield: JSOT Press, 1980), 420; and John A. Ziesler, "The Role of the Tenth Commandment in Romans 7," *JSNT* 10.33 (1988): 41–56.

7. E.g., Austin Busch, "The Figure of Eve in Romans 7:5–25," *BibInt* 12 (2004): 1–36; Stefan Krauter, "Eva in Röm 7," *ZNTW* 99 (2007): 1–17.

ple, reworks Käsemann's line to say: "there is nothing in the passage which does not fit *Eve*, and everything fits *Eve* alone."[8] For one thing, whenever the word *deceive* echoes Genesis 3 in Paul's letters, the allusions are always appended to Eve's action and never Adam's. Elder argues that the apostle has already ushered Eve onto the stage in Romans 7:1–6, highlighting the mutual topics of (1) life and death, (2) union between man and woman, and (3) the transgression of a command. This is not even to mention the terms "flesh" and "bear fruit," which occur in both passages as well.[9] The *I* especially fits Eve when placed beside other caricatures of her in Jewish literature as a lamenting figure through whom evil entered the world.[10] Such a depiction of Eve also coheres with first century laments, which were "characteristically feminine speeches."[11]

My professor at the University of Tübingen used to say: "We all live in the shadow of Adam" (or, in his exact words, *Wir lieben alle im Schatten Adams*).[12] In this case, it seems we also live in Eve's. Either way, for Paul, the shadow of Adam and Eve have both been eclipsed by the light of the gospel. Now, as the apostle proclaims in 13:14, believers can put off the old man and woman, fig leaves and all, and clothe ourselves instead with the Lord Jesus Christ who removes our condemnation and covers our shame.[13]

---

8. Nicolas Elder, "'Wretch I Am!' Eve's Tragic Speech-in-Character in Romans 7:7–25," *JBL* 137 (2018): 748, emphasis added.

9. Elder, "Eve," 757.

10. E.g., Sir 25:24; 2 Bar. 48:42–43; Philo, *Opif.* 136–167; LAE 14.

11. Elder, "Eve," 755. Cf. Philo, *Leg.* 3.19–20.

12. Cf. Otfried Hofius, "Der Mensch im Schatten Adams: Römer 7,7–25a," in *Paulusstudien II*, WUNT 143 (Tübingen: Mohr Siebeck, 2002), 104–54.

13. Cf. N. T. Wright, *Paul and the Faithfulness of God*, 2 vols. (Minneapolis: Fortress, 2013), 2:1016.

8.2. ISRAEL INCOGNITO

Other scholars consider the wretch as the collective story of Israel.[14] For these interpreters, the context rings more of the golden calf debacle in Exodus 32 than it does the fall in Genesis 3. The tip-off is where Paul proclaims: "I would not have known what it is to covet if the law had not said, Do not covet" (Rom 7:7 CSB). In this interpretation, Paul seeks to show how from Israel's start on Mount Sinai, she had failed to be faithful to the Lord. Ever since that no good very bad day, Israel had been riddled with death and defeat because she continued to disobey.[15]

Echoes of her storied history of failing to keep God's law run throughout Romans as well. For instance, in Romans 1, the notion of people trading the glory of God for that of animals also conjures up the golden calf fiasco.[16] And, according to Moo, when Paul pens Romans 7, he still has Moses and the law in mind from Romans 5. For example, as Paul argued there that sin was dormant from Adam to Moses in 5:13, so he does with the *ego* in 7:8.

---

14. Jackson Wu, *Reading Romans with Eastern Eyes: Honor and Shame in Paul's Message and Mission* (Downers Grove, IL: IVP Academic, 2019), 132–33.

15. See Joseph R. Dodson, "Rejection and Redemption in the Wisdom of Solomon and the Letter of Barnabas," *CBQ* 80 (2018): 45–61.

16. See Dunn, *Romans*, 61; Alec J. Lucas, "Reorienting the Structural Paradigm and Social Significance of Romans 1:18–32," *JBL* 131 (2012): 121–41.

Sin was in the world before the law, but sin is not charged to a person's account when there is no law. Nevertheless, death reigned from Adam to *Moses*. … The law came along to multiply the trespass. (5:13–14a, 20 CSB, emphasis added)	I would not have known what it is to covet if the law had not said, Do not covet. And sin, seizing an opportunity through the commandment, produced in me coveting of every kind. For apart from the law sin is dead. (7:7–8 CSB)

Since Jewish interpreters frequently associated Adam's fall in the garden with Israel's sin on the mountain,[17] Wright concludes that Paul here weaves together the story of Israel at Sinai with the story of Adam in Eden. Wright expounds that this represents "a classical rabbinic-style move, allowing two great scriptural narratives to interpret one another and to generate a third."[18] Regarding that third narrative, many scholars who see the *I*-figure as Adam, Eve, and/or Israel contend that the apostle expands one or more of these characters, so that the *I* goes on to represent someone sharing their predicament, such as the apostle himself before he met Christ.

8.3. NOT THE MAN I USED TO BE: PAUL BEFORE HE MET CHRIST

In 1932, Rudolf Bultmann concluded that the questions concerning the identity of the *ego* had been so sufficiently discussed that "the answer cannot be doubted." The *I*-figure, he declares,

---

17. See Wedderburn, "Adam," 413–30.

18. Wright, *Faithfulness of God*, 2:1014, 1017.

is a man under the law described from "the viewpoint of one who, through Christ, has been set free from the Law."[19] In short, the *I*-figure is "a Christian take on pre-Christian existence."[20]

A good number of scholars follow Bultmann's lead. For example, Troels Engberg-Pedersen avers that it is "established that Paul is describing an experience of living under the Mosaic Law as seen from the Christ-believing perspective."[21]

Many consider this to be Paul "reframing his own past through the prism of faith."[22] C. H. Dodd, for instance, refers to Romans 7:14–25 as Paul's "authentic transcript" of his pre-Christian life given to prove that believers are free from the dominion of sin.[23] Blinded by the light of the gospel, the apostle came to see the limit of the law, the folly of his zeal, and the emptiness of his former boasts. Now Paul, stripped of his former illusions, expounds upon his own dramatic dilemma, detailing the defeat he faced when he lived under the law. This position often sees Paul as seamlessly intertwining his pre-Christian life with Adam and Israel's story so that he stands as their representative in order to show solidarity with the history of his people. As Simon Gathercole writes, with the *ego*, "there are echoes not only of Israel's experience, but also

---

19. Rudolf Bultmann, *Exegetica: Aufsätze zur Erforschung des Neuen Testaments* (Tübingen: Mohr Siebeck, 1967), 198.

20. Ben Witherington III and Jason A. Myers, *Voices and Views on Paul: Exploring Scholarly Trends* (Downers Grove, IL: IVP Academic, 2020), 51.

21. Troels Engberg-Pedersen, "The Reception of Greco-Roman Culture in the New Testament: The Case of Romans 7:7–25," in *The New Testament as Reception*, ed. Mogens Müller and Henrik Tronier, JSNTSup 230 (London: Sheffield Academic, 2002), 37.

22. Antoon Vergote, "Vie, loi et clivage du Moi dans l'épître aux Romains 7," in *Exégèse et Herméneutique*, ed. Roland Barthes and Paul Beauchamps (Paris: Seuil, 1971), 121. See also Jewett, *Romans*, 444.

23. Dodd, *Romans*, 108. See also Lambrecht, *Wretched*, 90–91.

of Adam and Eve, in such a way that Paul's own pre-Christian biography is also drawn in."[24]

Extending beyond Israel's past, Paul may also be using the *I*-figure to relate to his other Jewish kinsfolk in their present situation under the law.[25] Looking back to his former life under the law from this new perspective, Paul demonstrates he can sympathize with any of his people who find themselves in the wretch's condition.[26] Because of the gospel, he can see clearly now that Christ had come to do what the law was powerless to do: to liberate him and his fellow Jews from the reign of sin. Perhaps this is an example of the apostle becoming all things to all people, becoming like one under the law to win those under the law (1 Cor 9:20). Even though Paul insists elsewhere that he has been liberated from the law, he likely takes a card out of the Hebrew confession deck here to depict himself as one in the flesh and under the law.[27]

In sum, to borrow from John Goodrich, Paul uses the *ego* to write himself back into Israel's story by placing "a retrospective and representative version of himself" at its core.[28] The good news is through Christ, God has made good on his promise to

---

24. Simon J. Gathercole, "Sin in God's Economy: Agencies in Romans 1 and 7," in *Divine and Human Agency in Paul and His Cultural Environment*, ed. John M. G. Barclay and Simon Gathercole, LNTS 335 (London: T&T Clark, 2006), 160. See also, Chester, "Retrospective View," 73; Wright, "Romans," 571–72.

25. Lambrecht, *Wretched*, 64; and Keener, *Mind*, 67. Cf. Phillip F. Esler, *Conflict and Identity in Romans: The Social Setting of Paul's Letter* (Minneapolis: Fortress, 2003), 242.

26. Moo, *Romans*, 474–76.

27. Mark Seifrid, "The Subject of Rom 7:14–25," *NovT* 34 (1992): 313–33. My favorite example of this is found in John K. Goodrich, "Sold under Sin: Echoes of Exile in Romans 7:14–25," *NTS* 59 (2013): 476–95. Goodrich shows how Paul also engages Isa 49–50 to present his preconversion life as an embodiment of unbelieving Israel, who had been sold as slaves because of their sins (Isa 50:1). Cf. Marc Philonenko, "Sur l'expression 'vendu au péché' dans l'Epître aux Romains,'" *RHR* 103 (1986): 41–52.

28. Goodrich, "Sold," 493.

deliver Israel from Adam's plight, for which, in Romans 7, Paul provides his pre-Christian self as the case in point (cf. 11:1–2).

8.4. AN ALMOST CHRISTIAN: CONVICTION NOT CONVERSION

While scholars do not tend to give much consideration to this view, some argue the *I*-figure represents a person *en route* to conversion.[29] For instance, Johann Albrecht Bengel concludes that rather than of Paul's own precipitous encounter with the Lord, the apostle speaks "*under the figure of a man*" engaged in the contest of conversion.[30] For Bengal, Romans 7 presents "the whole process of a man, in his transition from his state under the law to his state under grace, thinking, striving, and struggling forth."[31] This feeling of conviction finally reaches the tipping point when the wretch has a breakthrough and cries out for salvation. According to Bengel, this becomes the very moment of the *ego*'s mystical death with Christ, so that the *I* may now live in the newness of life.[32] Along these lines, Martyn Lloyd-Jones argues that Paul describes here a person neither unregenerate or regenerate but who, under the conviction of sin, feels utterly condemned at their unsuccessful attempt to keep the law. For Lloyd-Jones, such people are under "conviction but not conversion."[33]

---

29. See, however, Chad O. Brand, "Conclusion: Theological and Pastoral Issues," in Wilder, *Perspectives on Our Struggle*, 177–201.

30. Johann Albrecht Bengel, *Gnomon of the New Testament*, trans. A. R. Fausset, 5 vols. (Edinburgh, T&T Clark, 1858–1859), 3:92 (emphasis original).

31. Bengel, *Gnomon*, 3:91–92.

32. Bengel, *Gnomon*, 3:95–96; Chester, "Retrospective View," 64.

33. Martyn Lloyd-Jones, *Romans*, 14 vols. (Grand Rapids: Zondervan, 1973), 6:229. Stott considers the *I* as referring to Jewish Christians, like the disciples before Pentecost, for whom it "took time to adjust to the transition from the old aeon to the new" (Stott, *Romans*, 209).

8.5. PAUL'S INTERLOCUTOR

Romans 7 may not be the first time Paul evokes the *ego*. From as early as his "But what about you, O man" in Romans 2, the apostle picks a fight with an opponent scholars call an interlocutor.[34] The original audience would arguably call to mind the shots fired at the man who says he relies on the law. But Paul scolds the guy: "You who boast in the law, do you dishonor God by breaking the law?" And again, "God's name is blasphemed among the Gentiles because of you" (2:23–24). Here he also pits life "in the flesh" and "by the letter" over against "the Spirit" as he does in 7:5–6.[35]

Romans 2:28–29 (NASB, emphasis added)	Romans 7:5–6 (NASB, emphasis added)
For he is not a Jew who is one outwardly, nor is circumcision that which is outward in the *flesh*. But he is a Jew who is one inwardly; and circumcision is that which is of the heart, *by the Spirit, not by the letter*.	For while we were in the *flesh*, the sinful passions ... were at work. ... But now we have been released from the Law ... so that we serve in *newness of the Spirit* and not in *oldness of the letter*.

Many interpreters do not consider it a stretch to connect this interlocutor in Romans 2 to the wretch in Romans 7, since

---

34. For more on this, see Joseph R. Dodson, "The Yonder Man and the Hypocrite in Seneca's Epistle 59 and Paul's Letter to the Romans" *Religions* 14 (2023): 235, https://doi.org/10.3390/rel14020235.

35. See Wells, *Grace*, 224.

the former trusts in and teaches the law but does not obey it.[36]
Jipp, for example, links this hypocrite not only to the *I*-figure
in 7:14–25 but also to the men in 16:17 whom Paul lashes out
at for spreading doctrines contrary to the teaching that the
church had learned.[37] In this case, Paul's use of the *I* fits the
primary purpose of speech-in-character, which was, according to Quintilian, to air the thoughts of an adversary as though
he were talking to himself (*Inst.* 9.2.30–33). For this reading,
the apostle has these opponents in his rhetorical crosshairs
throughout the letter, and the *ego* in Romans 7 is another mis-
sile in that attack.

8.6. ANYONE UNDER THE LAW

For some, the *I* portrays anyone in general and no one in particular, for "all have sinned and fall short of the glory of God"
(Rom 3:23). From this perspective, the apostle seeks to depict
anyone who relies on themselves when attacked by sin and
who attempts to overcome it "under their own steam."[38] As a
result, like the wretch, they too experience moral frustration
and spiritual disaster.

Several scholars rightly push back at this view, though, since
it has a tendency to lose sight of the context of Romans 7 and
disregards "the specific emphasis Paul places upon the inter-
action of the 'I' with the Mosaic law."[39] As Moo argues, Paul's
address to "those who know the law" in 7:1 signifies that what
he seeks to explain is not a timeless and universal experience

---

36. McKnight, *Romans*, 173. The man's attitude in ch. 2, though, is unlike the *ego*'s
humility in ch. 7.

37. Jipp, "Educating," 231–57.

38. Longenecker, *Romans*, 620.

39. Kruse, *Romans*, 316.

but one "restricted to those who live under the Law of Moses."[40]
Also, it is the Mosaic law that is said to prompt sin, *not* Paul's
teaching of the law of Christ or of his preaching about faith.
These gospel lessons produce righteous obedience instead (1:5;
13:9–10). Over against the wretch and his partial fealty to the
law, believers have come to obey from their hearts the pattern
of teaching the apostle handed down to them, which has now
claimed their allegiance (6:17).[41]

With this in mind, Maston improves upon this interpretation, concluding that the *ego* represents *anyone who lives under
the Torah* and strives to keep its commandments.[42] Along these
lines, taking the immediate historical context into account, Bird
and Lee see the wretch as not only a rehearsal of the story of
Adam, unbelieving Israel, and preconversion Paul, but also as a
marked warning to any Jewish believer, God-fearer, and prose-
lyte in the church tempted to live under the Mosaic law rather
than by the Holy Spirit.[43]

8.7. IT'S MORE COMPLICATED:
A CHRISTIAN'S EXPERIENCE BUT
NOT A CHRISTIAN EXPERIENCE

Will Timmins considers this whole debate as hampered by
the imposing of a Christian versus pre-Christian framework
onto Romans 7.[44] He argues the situation instead represents

---

40. Douglas J. Moo, "Israel and Paul in Romans 7.7–12," *NTS* 32 (1986): 124–25;
Kruse, *Romans*, 3; Wells, *Grace*, 240.

41. Ziesler, "Commandment," 51–52.

42. Maston, *Agency*, 132. Cf. Seifrid, "Romans 7," 115.

43. Bird, *Romans*, 235. Lee, *Paul's Gospel*, 353. Cf. Jewett, *Romans*, 444; Lambrecht,
Wretched, 90–91.

44. Timmins, *Romans 7*, 205.

"a *Christian's* experience" not a "*Christian* experience."[45] For Timmins, with the former, Paul provides a paradigm for how believers remain incapacitated in a "condition of fleshliness," and how they should remain keenly aware that in their own strength they stand impotent against indwelling sin.[46] For this reason, Christians need to confess their ongoing inability to do any good without God.[47]

On the other hand, in comparison to the inherent weakness displayed in Romans 7, *Christian* experience is that of a believer walking in the Spirit as seen in Romans 8.[48] Thus, following Timmins, Schreiner infers that we should not read the entirety of the Christian experience from the account in Romans 7, "for, as chapter 8 shows, believers by the power of the Spirit are enabled to keep God's law."[49] And again, "We should *not* conclude … that believers are utterly helpless under the power of sin, for this would leave out Rom 6 and 8."[50] In brief, according to this perspective, with this passage, Paul makes us grasp our own profound incapacities outside of life in Christ and underlines "the absolute necessity of serving in the 'newness of the Spirit' and no longer in the 'oldness of the letter.'"[51]

Due to the prevailing importance of Romans 6 and 8 for the Christian life, we should be careful not to mistake "*the*

---

45. Timmins, *Romans 7*, 205 (emphasis original).

46. Will Timmins, "What's Really Going On in Romans 7," https://www.thegospelcoalition.org/article/romans-7-apostle-paul-confession/.

47. See also Schreiner, *Romans*, 389: "When believers contemplate their own capacities, it is clear that they do not have the resources to do what God demands."

48. Timmins, *Romans 7*, 205.

49. Schreiner, *Romans*, 389.

50. Schreiner, *Romans*, 390.

51. Timmins, *Romans 7*, 199; and Timmins, "What's Really Going On." See also Garland, *Romans*, 233; and Morris, *Romans*, 291.

Christian's experience" for "the *Christian* experience," which can happen if we acknowledge our own impotence to conquer sin but stop short of surrendering to the Spirit's capacity to do so for us. In other words, this reading should not lead us to bemoan our defeated identity in Adam as much as to bask more than ever in our surpassing union and participation with the Lord.

8.8. CONCLUSION

We have now surveyed seven options for whom Paul might be describing in Romans 7. As for us, we think Paul depicts here his preconversion experience in light of the gospel and that he does so by going back to his roots, as far back as Adam and Eve, while particularly alluding to the story of Israel, his people "according to the flesh" (9:3 ESV). Even if you do not follow our view, we hope these options muddy the water enough to show the wretch is *clearly not* Paul as a miserable, fleshly believer and, by extension, not meant to be a representative of a normal Christian life constantly frustrated and defeated by sin. For this reason, we should base our understanding of our current relationship with sin on those texts that undoubtedly address this topic more than on a passage as controversial as 7:14–25. The best views of Romans 7 share the conviction that Paul means the miserable creature's experience to represent the believer's past rather than her present, since now, to borrow from the popular hymn "How Deep the Father's Love for Us," by grace alone, through faith alone, Christ has made "a wretch [God's] treasure."

Conclusion

The Purpose of the Ego

We began this book with a brief survey of two broad readings regarding the identity of the *I* in Romans 7:14–25: the Not Paul and the Totally Paul interpretations. Throughout we have argued against the popular rendition of the latter view, which considers Paul to be using the *ego* to depict the typical Christian life perpetually frustrated and foiled by sin. We went on to show how this view contradicts what the apostle wrote in Romans 6 and 8 as well as the verses in chapter 7 that introduce the wretch's monologue. Next, we described how this interpretation clashes with what the apostle wrote in his other letters about himself and the Christian relationship with sin.

We then dealt with the common objections from the Totally Paul proponents in the hopes of demonstrating that Romans 7 should not do the load-bearing work for understanding a believer's relationship with sin. We also surveyed possible identities of the *I*-figure: Adam and Eve, unbelieving Israel, preconversion Paul, the interlocutor, everyone tempted to live under the law rather than in the Spirit, or as a *Christian's* experience but not a *Christian* experience. Now, we would like to provide some possible reasons for why Paul used the *I* in the first place. The apostle's aim could have been (1) apocalyptic, (2) apologetic, (3) historical, (4) polemical, or (5) pastoral. Of course, Paul might have had a number of these purposes in mind as he penned this chapter.

One school of thought considers the apostle to be using the *I* for an *apocalyptic* reason. Gaventa, for example, concludes that, in light of Paul's focus on the figure of sin introduced in Romans 5, the chief concern of Romans 7 is "neither the Law nor the 'I' but the way in which Sin's power can reach into and use even the holy and right and good Law of God."[1] In this case, instead of an individual's struggle with pet sins, Romans 7 features the wretch and the law as pawns in an apocalyptic, cosmic war between the power of sin and the resurrected Lord. From this perspective, the *ego* "provides a showcase for the liberating power of Christ," who came into humanity to establish his kingdom and condemn the sin that had exploited the law.[2] This reading of Romans 7 brings in the wider context of Pauline thought and warns the reader to not be so self-absorbed that she makes this passage more about her individual problems than the inspiring narrative of the gospel. In this instance, Paul intends for us to garner from this passage two self-evident truths: the Cosmic Lord has conquered sin and redeemed his people. (Amen!)

---

1. Gaventa, "The Shape of the 'I,'" 77. See also Paul W. Meyer, "The Worm at the Core of the Apple: Exegetical Reflections on Romans 7," in *The Conversation Continues: Studies in Paul and John in Honor of J. Louis Martyn*, ed. Robert T. Fortna and Beverly R. Gaventa (Nashville: Abingdon, 1990), 62–84. Cf. Dodson, *"Powers" of Personification*, 123–39.

2. Dodd, *Paradigmatic*, 231.

Most scholars infer that Paul uses the *I*-figure with an *apologetic* goal in mind. As mentioned before, according to this view, Romans 7 seeks to defend the law and to let it off the hook for its unwanted partnership with sin. Therefore, as Stendahl puts it, the apostle primarily concerns himself here with the Mosaic law, not man's cloven ego or predicament—his own or otherwise.[3] Along similar lines (and often overlapping), other scholars consider the apostle's goal as *historical*, particularly related to Israel's circumstances. In this case, Romans 7 is not about Paul's individual introspective struggle with sin but regards his nation's precarious situation under it. Nonetheless, the apostle delights to share that Israel's tragic condition as depicted in the wretch's monologue now has a lasting solution. The resurrected Messiah, son of God, and holy seed of David has accomplished for her what the law could not. He, the *telos* of the law, has drawn near to his people to fulfill God's promise to Isaiah: anyone who calls on the Lord will not be put to shame (see Rom 10:4–11).

Both the apologetic and historical goals reveal how Protestants are so vain we probably thought the *I* was about us. We have possibly culturally appropriated a passage focused on the Mosaic law and the redemption of the people of Israel "whom he foreknew" (11:2).[4] But, in contrast to non-Jewish believers today who appeal to the wretch to explain their sinful habits, Paul uses the *I*-figure to read himself into Israel's story to weep and hope for the unredeemed. So, whereas the apocalyptic view reminds us to read Romans 7 with a gospel lens, the apologetic and historic goals remind us to read it with Hebrew eyes.

---

3. Stendahl, "Paul," 211. Cf. Maston, *Agency*, 127.

4. Cf. Wu, *Reading Romans*, and E. Randolph Richards and Richard James, *Misreading Scripture with Individualistic Eyes: Patronage, Honor, and Shame in the Biblical World* (Downers Grove, IL: IVP Academic, 2020).

As mentioned in the last chapter, Jipp connects Romans 7 with Romans 2 and Romans 16 to provide evidence of Paul's concern with those in Rome encouraging other believers to live under the law.[5] So also, McKnight sees within the *ego* the judgmental man from Romans 2 who is associated with the weak believers in Romans 13–14. According to McKnight, these who are preoccupied with Torah observance seek to persuade the strong to live under the law too. From this perspective, Paul's construal of the wretch's agony becomes "Paul's fullest argument against the need of the Torah for gentile converts."[6] If this sounds familiar, it is because Paul dealt with a similar problem in Galatia.[7] As in Galatians, his aim here may be part of larger *polemic* to confront people in the Roman church urging others to live according to the law, which in turn would lead them into the plight of the wretch rather than into the freedom of the Spirit. Related to the polemical purpose, as also discussed in the last chapter, scholars like Bird and Lee remind the reader of a likely *pastoral* aim. For them, more than *at* his opponents, Paul concentrates on their victims, who were being persuaded to live under the law even after beginning with the Spirit (see Gal 3:1–6).

As I was writing this conclusion, someone asked me what I was working on. When I told her it was about Romans 7, she quipped: "So you are writing a whole book on the chapter in the Bible that comes before everyone's favorite chapter in the Bible?" I laughed and agreed. I told her my reason for writing this book is to encourage believers to live into everyone's

---

5. Jipp, "Educating," 255.

6. McKnight, *Romans*, 173–74.

7. Martinus C. de Boer, "Sin and Soteriology in Romans," in *Sin and Its Remedy in Paul*, ed. Nijay K. Gupta and John K. Goodrich, Contours of Pauline Theology (Eugene, OR: Cascade, 2020), 21.

favorite chapter and not to get stuck in the one before it. So, whether you changed your mind or not and whichever view you adopt, we hope this book motivates you to come out of the "O what a wretch I am" funk and the "I cannot do what I want to do" resignation and fully lean into the promises of "everyone's favorite chapter" instead. We are not captives of sin but children of God. As the Father's heirs, we are no longer obligated to fulfill the desires of our flesh. Now, in Christ, we parade around as conquerors rather than march around in chains. And, as those who possess his indwelling Spirit, we can now mortify the misdeeds of our bodies and walk in freedom and newness of life. Perhaps gospel singer Donald Lawrence sums it up the best: how can I be a *slave* when the *Master* lives inside of me?[8]

8. Donald Lawrence, "He Heard My Cry: featuring Sir The Baptist & Arnetta Murrill-Crooms" on He Heard My Cry (Provident Label, 2017).

Afterword ~

Conquerors Not Captives

Romans 7 in the Life of the Believer

Martin Seligman performed an experiment in which he discovered that dogs whom he had previously shocked several times would eventually just lie down and absorb the bolts instead of jumping to freedom when the opportunity was given. This phenomenon became known as learned helplessness and is applied to a person who has experienced so much persistent failure she is conditioned to believe her situation is inescapable.[1] When it comes to sin, many believers suffer from a sort of learned helplessness. A person persuaded she will always be defeated by sin likely will be. People rarely win battles they are convinced they have already lost. Having been shocked by failure so many times, she feels powerless to change, so that—rather than living in the liberty of Romans 6 and 8— she remains in the misery of Romans 7, suffering sin's blows.

---

1. See https://www.verywellmind.com/what-is-learned-helplessness-2795326.

As mentioned throughout the book, although we disagree with the Totally Paul view that reads the plight of Romans 7 as the expectation for the ordinary Christian experience, we admit believers endure a real and steady struggle with temptation. We too give in to sin and, as a result, often feel its shock. However, significant theological difficulties and spiritual dangers rise from the position that presents believers as perpetually defeated by sin, sold as its slave, and unable to do good. First, this reading departs from the New Testament teaching regarding God's will for us to be holy, and it underestimates the Spirit's empowerment to conform us to the obedient image of Christ. Moreover, it overlooks God's provision of his body, the church, with whom we are transformed by the renewing of our minds as we offer our bodies as a living sacrifice, holy and pleasing to him.

But if Romans 7 is not talking about the typical experience of believers, what role does it play in our lives as believers? For one thing, rather than depicting the situation in which we are doomed to live, Romans 7 provides a rich description of the dreadful circumstances we have already been liberated from. As Origen put it, the experience of the miserable creature illustrates "to the utmost from how many evils and from how many kinds of death Christ has rescued us."[2] Thus, when we were like the miserable creature and could do nothing for God, God did everything for us, and for this we owe him thanks.[3] Now our declaration becomes less "Oh what a wretch I am" and more "Thanks be to God through our Lord Jesus Christ." Instead of moaning incessantly in our sin, we now exult in him, for

---

2. Origen, *Commentary on the Epistle to the Romans: Books 6–10*, trans. Thomas P. Scheck, Fathers of the Church (Washington, DC: Catholic University of America Press, 2002), 42.

3. Dodd, *Romans*, 116.

because of him, we are a new creation, his masterpiece and poem, made alive to do the good he prepared for us to do (Eph 2:10).

Second, Romans 7 adjures us to walk according to the Spirit and not to live under the law like the wretch. To say Romans 7 depicts an unbeliever does not mean it is impossible for believers to fall back into that perilous condition under the power of sin. This possibility leads to Paul's imperatives to the believers in Romans 6 not to let sin reign in their mortal bodies as well as to his warning in Romans 8 for them not to live in the flesh but to put to death its misdeeds.

Often when we refute the popular view of Romans 7, people respond by saying: Well, if this is true, then why does my life still look so much like that passage? Of course, it is difficult to answer this question since every person is different. And we want to be deeply sensitive to each individual situation. So, the answer requires at least a whole book on its own. Nevertheless, we will respond here with a humble discussion centered around four words: clarity, cultivation, confession, and counseling.

10.1. CLARITY

To riff on Socrates, if the unexamined life is not worth living, the unexamined faith is not worth having. Whereas the philosopher admonished his students to work on their self-awareness, Paul exhorts his followers to work out their own salvation (Phil 2:12). The apostle does not seek to make believers doubt their salvation, though. He intends for them to inspect it and to clarify where their life does not line up with their calling. When believers engage in this, it may turn out that, upon further investigation, they happily find they have indeed grown in godliness more than they previously realized. Although not as much as they still hope, they discover that their faith has

produced obedience, that their love has resulted in righteousness, and that their walk is more in step with the Spirit than
when they first believed (Rom 1:5; Phil 1:9–11; Gal 5:25). As
Kyle Fischer, one of my former students, concluded, "it's better
to measure my spiritual growth by decades more than by days."

A believer might also need to clarify the difference between
facing temptations and falling into sin. The more a person
matures in Christ, the more intensely she may have to fight
against the temptations she once groveled to. But temptation
is not sin. This relates to Augustine's view, which considered
the *ego*'s terrible cry as more about frustration with the temptation to do evil than actually doing evil. While self-control and
personal restraint are possible, a believer might still cry out
like the wretch because she too grows weary of being tempted
by the desire to sin in the first place.[4] Although we do not buy
Augustine's interpretation of Romans 7, if this is the way you
read the groaning of the *I*, then be encouraged. Look how far
you have come. Once you could not do any good at all, but
now, you just do not do it as perfectly as you would like. You
have moved from the bondage of always saying "yes" to sin to
a place of frustration because you have to keep telling it "no."

We do roundly affirm Wesley's clarification: just because sin
still resides with us does not mean sin still rules in us.[5] As we
continue to walk according to the Spirit, we will increasingly
do more good, more often, and more fully than we did at first.
Like an archer in training, we do not hit the mark every time,
but, by the grace of God, we hit it more than we used to. This
progress follows what Wesley wrote in his journal: "I was much
buffeted with temptations, but I cried out, and they fled away."

---

4. Augustine, "Treatise," 24.

5. "Sin in Believers," sermon 13.4.5–10, *WW* 5:152–54.

The temptations departed, he explains, because when he lifted his eyes to the Lord, the Lord sent "help from his holy place." Wesley finds clarity here—in the past when he fought against sin he was often defeated. But now, due to the Spirit working within him, he increasingly became the conqueror over sin more than the captive to it.[6]

This leads to another crucial point of clarification: we are not alone. Paul immediately follows the "work out your own salvation" command in Phil 2:12 with an affirmation: "For it is God who is working in you both to will and to work according to his good purpose" (2:13 CSB). If Lord is working for us, "Who can be against us?" (Rom 8:31). And if God is working *for* us, he is also working *in* us. And if he is working *in* us, he is also praying *through* us, helping us in our weakness and groaning in our pain (8:26–27).

Luther tells us what happens when God's Spirit prays through us and intercedes on our behalf. According to Luther, the power of sin, the weakness of the flesh, the darts of the devil, and the agues of death, all cry out against us. In concert, the law scolds, sin screams, death thunders, and the devil roars. But, "in the midst of the clamor, the Spirit of Christ cries in our hearts." And this little cry, Luther concludes, transcends the howl and "hullabaloo" of them all.[7] In response to this call for help, God sends his aid from his holy place so that, to quote Charles Spurgeon, now "in fighting with sin," we are "waging Jehovah's war," before whom all "the hordes of evil shall fly."

---

6. "The Journal of John Wesley, May 24, 1738," *WW* 1:98–104.

7. Martin Luther, *Commentary on the Epistle to the Galatians*, trans. and condensed by Theodore Graebner (Grand Rapids: Zondervan, 1939), ch. 4 v. 6, 159.

Therefore, Spurgeon cheers, quail not, shrink not, flinch not: for the battle is the Lord's.[8]

10.2. CULTIVATION

Many believers know the familiar promise "Delight yourself in the LORD; And He will give you the desires of your heart" (Ps 37:4 NASB). What is sometimes neglected, however, is the command immediately preceding this promise, which calls God's people to "cultivate faithfulness" (Ps 37:3 NASB). As the psalmist demonstrates, faithfulness does not just happen, it takes digging, weeding, planting, and watering. Whereas God does promise to make "our righteousness shine like the dawn," he also invites us to work with him, putting seeds of righteousness in the ground so that he can make them grow (Ps 37:6; cf. Phil 1:9–11).

This notion of "cultivating faithfulness" reminds us of Paul's entreaty to Timothy: "train yourself for godliness" (1 Tim 4:7). Whereas the psalmist goes with the horticultural metaphor to talk about moral progression, Paul draws upon activities associated with the gymnasium to enjoin Timothy to be an example for others in speech, conduct, love, faith, and purity (4:12). To do so, however, Timothy must cultivate faithfulness and train himself for godliness. Around the same time Paul penned this, the Stoic philosopher Seneca also appealed to athletic imagery to discuss growing in virtue. Although sports metaphors have become tired and threadbare in our society, Seneca's extension of the illustration beyond what Paul wrote has proven helpful to us.

---

8. Charles Spurgeon, *Morning and Evening Daily Devotions*, 2nd ed. (London: Passmore & Alabaster, 1896), Morning, June 8.

The Stoic argues that all athletes require different strokes for their particular training. There is the rare athlete who is so self-disciplined she gets up by herself and pushes herself to the max with little to no help from others. The Stoic continues, though. There are more athletes who are not like this. Instead, they need the fellowship and accountability of a training partner. These people struggle to get up or to push themselves without having someone to do it with them. Finally, Seneca avers, most athletes need more than a training partner to achieve their potential. They need a coach to bark them out of bed, to encourage them with affirming words, and even, at times, to become like a drill sergeant to push them beyond what they thought possible. Whichever the case, the Stoic warns of training for godliness with "too trifling a spirit." For, he quips, it is very difficult to progress in virtue when the only time we set aside for learning how to overcome our vices is the little time we have left over from indulging them.

As we examine our lives in the hopes of cultivating faithfulness and training for godliness, we may find areas where, like the first athlete, we progress without needing much support. But there are likely other situations where we need someone to come alongside us, to spot us, and to cheer us on. Finally, there is probably an area or two where we need a coach to hold our feet to the fire, especially when we would prefer to relax and indulge the very desires we were planning to train against. The places our lives match up with Romans 7 is likely where we need to call in backup, the severity of which will determine whether we need a personal trainer or a drill sergeant.

In sum, winning does not come from trying harder, but from cultivating more and training better. Yet, in doing so, rather than condemning ourselves when we fail, we need to be patient with ourselves and not do it alone. The pursuit of godliness is a group effort not a solo run. Together we hold to the promises that he who began a good work in us will bring it to completion and that his love covers the multitude of our failures (Phil 1:6; Jas 5:20).

10.3. CONFESSION

Speaking of loved ones and failures, James concludes his letter commanding believers to confess theirs to one another so that they can be healed. For James, the remedy to bondage from our sin includes confessing our sins to others. Although many of us do this in some fashion, we tend to avoid confessing our specific, hidden sins. Instead, we keep our confession so general it is too weak and wobbly to do much good. In *Life Together*, Dietrich Bonhoeffer explains why baring our souls and confessing our precise sins to others is necessary. He writes: "By confessing actual sins the old self dies a painful, humiliating death before the eyes of another Christian."[9] Why is it easier to confess our sin to a holy God than it is to a fellow sinner? It seems it would be just the opposite. Perhaps it is that the transcendent God often feels so abstract, far and away, that our confessions also come out as insubstantial.[10] However, when we open up to a Christian sister or brother who stand as a concrete representation of God, we feel vulnerable, naked, and exposed—the exact conditions the Lord requires to work liberation in our lives.

Also notice what Paul says in Galatians 6:1–2 just after his discussion about Christians crucifying their sins. When someone falls, she should be gently restored by fellow believers because we need each other to overcome our sins. When Paul

---

9. Dietrich Bonhoeffer, *Life Together* (San Francisco: Harper & Row, 1978), 89.

10. For more on this, see Kelly M. Kapic, *Embodied Hope: A Theological Meditation on Pain and Suffering* (Downers Grove, IL: IVP Academic, 2017), 140–48.

calls us to crucify our flesh, he does not conceive of an individual nailing her own greed or lust or pride to a single cross in an isolated, private room. Instead, he has in mind the community of believers sincerely, patiently, and humbly helping each other do so. When the Romans crucified a person, they would often station a soldier at the bottom to make sure that whoever was on those beams did not come down until they were dead. As we look at our lives, this makes us wonder whom we have posted at the bottom of our cross to make sure our anger, selfishness, and jealousy are being put to death.[11] We, too, need someone we can trust to station herself before us so that we can detail to her our deepest, darkest sins. Then, and just as importantly, as a representative of God in bodily form, she prays the Lord's palpable forgiveness, freedom, and peace over our lives. And, as James puts it above, such a prayer is powerful and effective (Jas 5:16).

10.4. COUNSELING

When one of my children was around four years old, we had a group of college students over. I said to my older kids, "one of you go ask our guests who wants coffee and who wants tea." We were all surprised when the four year old bounded into our living room instead and blurted: "Raise your hand if you need therapy!" I am not sure how he got "therapy" from "coffee and tea," but we all had a good, albeit nervous, laugh. If we are honest, most of us should probably raise our hands to that question. While we all could use a good counselor in general, some of us may be fighting addictions and facing trauma that go way beyond what Paul is talking about in Romans 7. So, if our points about clarity, cultivation, and confession are

---

11. I am indebted to my former professor, Dr. Woo, for this insight.

not enough to get you from Romans 7 to Romans 8, perhaps the Lord wants to help you achieve additional freedom by his working through a therapist, a counselor, or a psychologist. As God uses medical doctors and medicines to heal our bodies, he often powerfully uses professional counselors, therapists, and psychologists to minister to our souls. We struggle to grow spiritually when we keep dragging along or ignoring the paralyzing parts of our past, to which these women and men have been called and trained to help us address. We all are broken and need various ways to overcome our struggles, so kindness and grace should be extended to everyone wherever they are on their journey. Perhaps you even need to extend kindness and grace to yourself by seeing a mental professional.

10.5. CONCLUSION

If a therapist were to diagnose the wretch in Romans 7, she might say he is caught up in what scientist call "rumination," an excessive thinking "around negative content that generates emotional discomfort."[12] Clinical rumination often manifests with a fixation on questions like "What's wrong with me?" and usually involves a person spiraling into a "dark whirlpool of negativity" so that she feels "hopeless, exhausted and depressed."[13] Sounds a lot like the *ego*. "There's nothing good in me." "I'm sold as a slave to sin." "I cannot do any good." "O what a miserable creature I am!"

---

12. Randy A. Sansone and Lori A. Sansone, "Rumination: Relationships with Physical Health," *Innovations in Clinical Neuroscience* 9.2 (2012): 29–34.

13. https://www.psychologytoday.com/us/blog/your-personal-renaissance /201309/the-healing-power-beauty. See also Mark Williams et al., *The Mindful Way through Depression: Freeing Yourself from Chronic Unhappiness* (New York: Guilford, 2007).

For treating rumination, psychologists have developed a therapy called rumination-focused cognitive-behavioral therapy.[14] Although it is more complicated, the gist is to shift the patient from *unhelpful* rumination to *helpful* rumination. With respect to Romans 7, perhaps the wretch's problem is that he is ruminating on the wrong person. Instead of "I … I … I … me … me … me," he needs to fixate on "Jesus, Jesus, Jesus."

Therefore, we must not, like the wretch, ruminate on our own failings instead of the love of God that has been abundantly poured into our hearts. Liberation from the *ego*'s predicament involves us being fixed more on our Lord and less on our sin—less on our condition as a miserable creature in Adam and more on our status as a new creation in Christ. To draw from C. S. Lewis, we only learn to behave ourselves when we forget ourselves, caught up in the kind worship that made King David dance.[15] In other words, when we focus on the Lord, who is our life and our identity, in whom we are hidden and secure, our failings in this world grow strangely dim in the light of his glory and grace. The more we ruminate on him, the more we delight in him, and the more we dance as he gives us the desires of our heart, so that, unlike the wretch, we can finally do the things we want to do. And to this we say: "Thanks be to God through our Lord Jesus Christ!"

---

14. Edward R. Watkins et al., "Rumination-Focused Cognitive-Behavioural Therapy for Residual Depression: Phase II Randomised Controlled Trial," *British Journal of Psychiatry* 199 (2011): 317–22.

15. C. S. Lewis, *Reflections on the Psalms* (Princeton: Recording for the Blind & Dyslexic, 2007), 45. Along these lines, Packer comments: "The life of true holiness is rooted in the soul of awed adoration … no blend of zeal, passion, self-denial, discipline, orthodoxy, and effort adds up to holiness where praise is lacking." J. I. Packer, *Rediscovering Holiness* (Secunderabad: OM Books, 2004), 73.

Our Father in Heaven, hallowed be your name among us
that together we live lives worthy of your gracious
    calling upon us,
in honor of your Son's sacrifice for us,
and empowered by your Spirit dwelling within us.

Bibliography ∼

Ambrosiaster. *Commentarius in Epistolam ad Romanos*
    81.1.74–75.

Anderson, R. Dean. *Ancient Rhetorical Theory and Paul.*
    CBET 18. Kampen: Kok Pharos, 1996.

Augustine. "A Treatise against Two Letters of the Pelagians."
    NPNF 1/5:24.

Barclay, John M. G. *Paul and the Gift.* Grand Rapids:
    Eerdmans, 2015.

———. *Obeying the Truth: Paul's Ethics in Galatians.*
    Minneapolis: Fortress, 1988.

Beker, Johan Christiaan. *The Triumph of God: The Essence of
    Paul's Thought.* Minneapolis: Fortress, 1990.

Bengel, Johann Albrecht. *Gnomon of the New Testament.*
    Translated by A. R. Fausset. 5 vols. Edinburgh: T&T
    Clark, 1858–1859.

Bird, Michael F. *Romans.* Story of God Bible Commentary.
    Grand Rapids: Zondervan, 2016.

Black, Matthew. *Romans.* NCB. Grand Rapids: Eerdmans,
    1984.

Boer, Martinus C. de. "Sin and Soteriology in Romans."
    Pages 14–32 in *Sin and Its Remedy in Paul.* Edited by
    Nijay K. Gupta and John K. Goodrich. Contours of
    Pauline Theology. Eugene, OR: Cascade, 2020.

Bonhoeffer, Dietrich. *Life Together*. San Francisco: Harper & Row, 1978.

Bounds, Christopher T. "Augustine's Interpretation of Romans 7:14–25." Pages 15–27 in *The Continuing Relevance of Wesleyan Theology: Essays in Honor of Laurence W. Wood*. Edited by Nathan Crawford. Eugene, OR: Pickwick, 2011.

Brand, Chad O. "Conclusion: Theological and Pastoral Issues." Pages 177–201 in *Perspectives on Our Struggle with Sin: Three Views of Romans 7*. Edited by Terry L. Wilder. Nashville: B&H Academic, 2011.

Bray, Gerald L. *Romans*. ACCSNT 6. Downers Grove, IL: InterVarsity Press, 1998.

Brown, Derek R. "'The God of Peace Will Shortly Crush Satan Under Your Feet': Paul's Eschatological Reminder in Romans 16:20a." *Neot* 44 (2010): 1–14.

Bruce, F. F. *The Epistle of Paul to the Romans: An Introduction and Commentary*. TNTC. Grand Rapids: Eerdmans, 1985.

Bultmann, Rudolf. *Exegetica: Aufsätze zur Erforschung des Neuen Testaments*. Edited by Erich Dinkler. Tübingen: Mohr Siebeck, 1967.

Bunyan, John. *Pilgrim's Progress*. New York: Hurst, 1903.

Busch, Austin. "The Figure of Eve in Romans 7:5–25." *BibInt* 12 (2004): 1–36.

Calvin, John. *Commentaries on the Epistle of Paul the Apostle to the Romans*. Translated and edited by John Owen. Edinburgh: Calvin Translation Society, 1849.

Chamblin, J. Knox. *Paul and the Self: Apostolic Teaching for Personal Wholeness*. Grand Rapids: Baker, 1993.

Chang, Hae-Kyung. "The Christian Life in a Dialectical Tension? Rom 7:7–25." *NovT* 49 (2007): 257–80.

Chester, Stephen. "The Retrospective View of Romans 7:
    Paul's Past in Present Perspective." Pages 57–102 in
    *Perspectives on Our Struggle with Sin: Three Views of
    Romans 7*. Edited by Terry L. Wilder. Nashville: B&H
    Academic, 2011.

Cohick, Lynn H. *Philippians*. Story of God Commentary.
    Grand Rapids: Zondervan, 2013.

Cranfield, C. E. B. *Romans: A Shorter Commentary*. Grand
    Rapids: Eerdmans, 1985.

Das, A. Andrew. *Paul, the Law, and the Covenant*. Peabody,
    MA: Hendrickson, 2001.

Dodd, Brian J. *Paul's Paradigmatic "I": Personal Example as
    Literary Strategy*. JSNTSup 177. Sheffield: Sheffield
    Academic, 1999.

Dodd, C. H. *The Epistle of Paul to the Romans*. MNTC. New
    York: Harper, 1932.

Dodson, Joseph R. "Paul and Seneca on the Cross: The
    Metaphor of Crucifixion in Galatians and *De Vita
    Beata*." Pages 247–66 in *Paul and Seneca in Dialogue*.
    Edited by Joseph R. Dodson and David E. Briones.
    Ancient Philosophy and Religion 2. Leiden: Brill, 2017.

———. *The "Powers" of Personification: Rhetorical Purpose in the
    "Book of Wisdom" and the Letter to the Romans*. BZNW
    161. Berlin: de Gruyter, 2008.

———. "Rejection and Redemption in the Wisdom of
    Solomon and the Letter of Barnabas." *CBQ* 80 (2018):
    45–61.

———. "The Yonder Man and the Hypocrite in Seneca's
    Epistle 59 and Paul's Letter to the Romans." *Religions*
    14 (2023): 235. https://doi.org/10.3390/rel14020235.

Dryden, J. de Waal. "Revisiting Romans 7: Law, Self, and
    Spirit." *JSPL* 5 (2015): 129–51.

Dunn, James D. G. "The Balance of Already/Not Yet: Romans 8:1–17." Pages 101–7 in *Preaching Romans: Four Perspectives*. Edited by Scot McKnight and Joseph B. Modica. Grand Rapids: Eerdmans, 2019.

———. *Romans*. 2 vols. WBC 38. Waco, TX: Word, 1988.

———. "Romans 7.14–25 in the Theology of Paul." *TZ* 31 (1975): 257–73.

Eastman, Susan Grove. *Paul and the Person*. Grand Rapids: Eerdmans, 2017.

Elder, Nicholas. "'Wretch I Am!' Eve's Tragic Speech-in-Character in Romans 7:7–25." *JBL* 137 (2018): 743–63.

Engberg-Pedersen, Troels. "The Reception of Greco-Roman Culture in the New Testament: The Case of Romans 7:7–25." Pages 32–57 in *The New Testament as Reception*. Edited by Mogens Müller and Henrik Tronier. JSNTSup 230. London: Sheffield Academic, 2002.

Epictetus. *The Discourse as Reported by Arrian, the Manual, and Fragments*. Translated by W. A. Oldfather. LCL. Cambridge: Harvard University Press, 1925.

Erasmus, Desiderius. *Annotations on Romans*. Translated by John B. Payne. CWE 56. Toronto: University of Toronto Press, 1994.

———. *Paraphrases on Romans and Galatians*. Edited by Robert D. Sider et al. CWE 42. Toronto: University of Toronto Press, 1984.

Esler, Philip F. *Conflict and Identity in Romans: The Social Setting of Paul's Letter*. Minneapolis: Fortress, 2003.

Fee, Gordon D. *God's Empowering Presence: The Holy Spirit in the Letters of Paul*. Peabody, MA: Hendrickson, 1994.

Garland, David. *Romans: An Introduction and Commentary*. TNTC 6. Downers Grove, IL: InterVarsity Press, 2021.

Gathercole, Simon J. "A Law unto Themselves: The Gentiles in Romans 2.14–15 Revisited." *JSNT* 24.85 (2002): 27–49.

———. "Sin in God's Economy: Agencies in Romans 1 and 7." Pages 158–72 in *Divine and Human Agency in Paul and His Cultural Environment*. Edited by John M. G. Barclay and Simon Gathercole. LNTS 335. London: T&T Clark, 2006.

Gaventa, Beverly Roberts. "The Shape of the 'I': The Psalter, the Gospel, and the Speaker in Romans 7." Pages 77–92 in *Apocalyptic Paul: Cosmos and Anthropos in Romans 5–8*. Edited by Beverly Roberts Gaventa. Waco, TX: Baylor University Press, 2013.

———. "The Singularity of the Gospel Revisited." Pages 187–99 in *Galatians and Christian Theology: Justification, the Gospel, and Ethics in Paul's Letter*. Edited by Mark W. Elliot, Scott J. Jafemann, N. T. Wright, and John Frederick. Grand Rapids: Baker Academic, 2014.

Goodrich, John K. "Sold under Sin: Echoes of Exile in Romans 7:14–25." *NTS* 59 (2013): 476–95.

Gorman, Michael J. *Romans: A Theological and Pastoral Commentary*. Grand Rapids: Eerdmans, 2022.

Grappe, Christian. "Qui me délivrera de ce corps de mort? L'esprit de vie! Romains 7,24 et 8,2 comme éléments de typologie adamique." *Bib* 83 (2002): 472–92.

Gregory, Horace, trans. *Ovid:The Metamorphosis*. London: Penguin, 1958.

Hayes, Christine. *What's Divine about Divine Law? Early Perspectives*. Princeton: Princeton University Press, 2015.

Heim, Erin M. *Adoption in Galatians and Romans: Contemporary Metaphor Theories and the Pauline Huiothesia Metaphors*. BibInt 153. Leiden: Brill, 2017.

Hofius, Otrfied. "Der Mensch im Schatten Adams: Römer 7,7–25a." Pages 104–54 in *Paulusstudien II*. WUNT 143. Tübingen: Mohr Siebeck, 2002.

Hooker, Morna D. "Adam in Romans 1." NTS 6 (1960): 297–306.

Hughes, R. Kent. *Luke: That You May Know the Truth*. Preaching the Word. Wheaton, IL: Crossway, 2015.

Jewett, Robert. *Romans: A Commentary*. Hermeneia. Minneapolis: Fortress, 2007.

Jipp, Joshua W. "Educating the Divided Soul in Paul and Plato: Reading Romans 7:7–25 and Plato's Republic." Pages 231–57 in *Paul: Jew, Greek, and Roman*. Edited by Stanley Porter. Pauline Studies 5. Leiden: Brill, 2008.

Jongkind, Dirk, Peter J. Williams, Peter M. Head, and Patrick James, eds. *The Tyndale House Greek New Testament*. Cambridge: Cambridge University Press, 2017.

Kapic, Kelly M. *Embodied Hope: A Theological Meditation on Pain and Suffering*. Downers Grove, IL: IVP Academic, 2017.

Käsemann, Ernst. *Commentary on Romans*. Translated by G. W. Bromiley. Grand Rapids: Eerdmans, 1980.

Keck, Leander E. *Romans*. ANTC. Nashville: Abingdon, 2005.

Keener, Craig S. *The Mind of the Spirit: Paul's Approach to Transformed Thinking*. Grand Rapids: Baker Academic, 2016.

Knox, John. *Life in Christ Jesus: Reflections on Romans 5–8*. New York: Seabury, 1961.

Krauter, Stefan. "Eva in Röm 7." *ZNTW* 99 (2007): 1–17.

Kruse, Collin G. *Paul's Letter to the Romans*. PNTC. Grand
     Rapids: Eerdmans, 2012.

Kümmel, Werner Georg. *Römer 7 und das Bild des Menschen
     im Neuen Testament: Zwei Studien*. Munich: Kaiser,
     1974.

Lambrecht, Jan. *The Wretched "I" and Its Liberation*. Grand
     Rapids: Eerdmans, 1992.

Lawrence, Donald. "He Heard My Cry: featuring Sir The
     Baptist & Arnetta Murrill-Crooms" on He Heard My
     Cry. Provident Label, 2017.

Lee, Jae Hyun. *Paul's Gospel in Romans: A Discourse Analysis
     of Rom 1:16–8:39*. Linguistic Biblical Studies 3. Leiden:
     Brill, 2010.

Lee, Max J. *Moral Transformation in Greco-Roman Philosophy
     of Mind: Mapping the Moral Milieu of the Apostle Paul
     and His Diaspora Jewish Contemporaries*. WUNT 2/515.
     Tübingen: Mohr Siebeck, 2020.

Lewis, C. S. *Reflections on the Psalms*. Princeton: Recording
     for the Blind & Dyslexic, 2007.

Lichtenberger, Hermann. *Das Ich Adams und das Ich der
     Menschheit: Studien zum Menschenbild in Römer 7*.
     WUNT 164. Tübingen: Mohr Siebeck, 2004.

Lloyd-Jones, D. Martyn. *Romans*. 14 vols. Grand Rapids:
     Zondervan, 1970–1986.

Longenecker, Bruce W. *Rhetoric at the Boundaries: The
     Art and Theology of the New Testament Chain-Link
     Transitions*. Waco, TX: Baylor University Press, 2005.

——. "Sin and the Sovereignty of God in Romans." Pages
     33–48 in *Sin and Its Remedy in Paul*. Edited by Nijay K.
     Gupta and John K. Goodrich. Eugene, OR: Cascade,
     2020.

Longenecker, Richard N. *The Epistle to the Romans: A Commentary on the Greek Text.* NIGTC. Grand Rapids: Eerdmans, 2016.

Lucas, Alec J. "Reorienting the Structural Paradigm and Social Significance of Romans 1:18–32." *JBL* 131 (2012): 121–41.

Luther, Martin. *Commentary on the Epistle to the Galatians.* Translated and condensed by Theodore Graebner. Grand Rapids: Zondervan, 1939.

———. *Commentary on Romans.* Grand Rapids: Kregel, 1982.

Maston, Jason. *Divine and Human Agency in Second Temple Judaism and Paul: A Comparative Study.* WUNT 2/297. Tübingen: Mohr Siebeck, 2010.

Mathewson, David, and Elodie Ballantine Emig. *Intermediate Greek Grammar: Syntax for Students of the New Testament.* Grand Rapids: Baker Academic, 2016.

McKnight, Scot. *Reading Romans Backwards.* Waco, TX: Baylor University Press, 2019.

Metzger, Bruce M. *A Textual Commentary on the Greek New Testament.* 2nd ed. New York: United Bible Societies, 1994.

Meyer, Paul W. "The Worm at the Core of the Apple: Exegetical Reflections on Romans 7." Pages 62–84 in *The Conversation Continues: Studies in Paul and John in Honor of J. Louis Martyn.* Edited by Robert T. Fortna and Beverly R. Gaventa. Nashville: Abingdon, 1990.

Moo, Douglas J. "Israel and Paul in Romans 7.7–12," *NTS* 32 (1986): 122–35.

———. *Romans.* NICNT. Grand Rapids: Eerdmans, 1996.

Morris, Leon. *The Epistle to the Romans.* PNTC. Grand Rapids: Eerdmans, 1994.

Myers, Jason A. *Paul, The Apostle of Obedience: Reading Obedience in Romans.* LNTS 668. London: T&T Clark, 2022.

Novenson, Matthew V. *Paul, Then and Now.* Grand Rapids: Eerdmans, 2022.

O'Connor, Flannery. "The Fiction Writer and His Country." Pages 25–35 in *Mystery and Manners: Occasional Prose.* Edited by Sally Fitzgerald and Robert Fitzgerald. New York: Farrar, Straus & Giroux, 1969.

Origen. *Commentary on the Epistle to the Romans: Books 6–10.* Translated by Thomas P. Scheck. Fathers of the Church. Washington, DC: Catholic University of America Press, 2002.

Osborne, Grant R. "The Flesh without the Spirit: Romans 7 and Christian Experience." Pages 6–48 in *Perspectives on Our Struggle with Sin: Three Views of Romans 7.* Edited by Terry L. Wilder. Nashville: B&H Academic, 2011.

Packer, J. I. *Rediscovering Holiness.* Secunderabad: OM Books, 2004.

———. "The Wretched Man Revisited: Another Look at Romans 7:14–25." Pages 70–81 in *Romans and the People of God: Essays in Honor of Gordon D. Fee on the Occasion of His 65th Birthday.* Edited by S. K. Soderlund and N. T. Wright. Grand Rapids: Eerdmans, 1999.

Palmer, Delano V. "Romans 7 Once Again: Intertextual Setting, Structure, and Rhetorical Strategy." *Caribbean Journal of Evangelical Theology* 16 (2017): 132–64.

Pate, C. Marvin. *Romans.* Teach the Text. Grand Rapids: Baker, 2013.

Payne, Don J. *Already Sanctified: A Theology of the Christian Life in Light of God's Completed Work*. Grand Rapids: Baker Academic, 2020.

Philonenko, Marc. "Sur l'expression 'vendu au péché' dans l'Epître aux Romains.'" *RHR* 103 (1986): 41–52.

Pitre, Brant, Michael P. Barber, and John A. Kincaid. *Paul: A New Covenant Jew; Rethinking Pauline Theology*. Grand Rapids: Eerdmans, 2019.

Plantinga, Cornelius. *Not the Way It's Supposed to Be: A Breviary of Sin*. Grand Rapids: Eerdmans, 1996.

Plato. *Republic*. Translated by Paul Shorey. 2 vols. LCL. Cambridge: Harvard University Press, 1930.

Reasoner, Mark. *Romans in Full Circle: A History of Interpretation*. Louisville: Westminster John Knox, 2005.

Romanello, Stefano. "Rom 7,7–25 and the Impotence of the Law: A Fresh Look at a Much-Debated Topic Using Literary-Rhetorical Analysis." *Bib* 84 (2003): 510–30.

Ryle, J. C. *Holiness: Its Nature, Hindrances, Difficulties, and Roots*. Carlisle: Banner of Truth, 2014.

Sansone, Randy A., and Lori A. Sansone. "Rumination: Relationships with Physical Health." *Innovations in Clinical Neuroscience* 9.2 (2012): 29–34.

Schreiner, Thomas R. *Romans*. 2nd ed. BECNT. Grand Rapids: Baker Academic, 2018.

Seifrid, Mark A. "Romans 7: The Voice of the Law, the Cry of Lament, and the Shout of Thanksgiving." Pages 111–76 in *Perspectives on Our Struggle with Sin: Three Views of Romans 7*. Edited by Terry L. Wilder. Nashville: B&H Academic, 2011.

———. "The Subject of Rom 7:14–25." *NovT* 34 (1992): 313–33.

Shogren, Gary S. "The 'Wretched Man' of Romans 7:14–25 as *Reductio ad absurdum*." EQ 72 (2000): 119–34.

Sprinkle, Preston M. *Law and Life: The Interpretation of Leviticus 18:5 in Early Judaism and in Paul*. WUNT 2/241. Tübingen: Mohr Siebeck, 2008.

Spurgeon, C. H. *Morning and Evening Daily Devotions*. 2nd ed. London: Passmore & Alabaster, 1896.

———. "The Way to Honor." Sermon no. 1118 in vol. 18 of *Metropolitan Tabernacle Pulpit: Sermons Preached and Revised by C.H. Spurgeon during the Year 1873*. London: Passmore & Alabaster, 1874.

Stendahl, Krister. "The Apostle Paul and the Introspective Conscience of the West." HTR 56 (1963): 199–215.

Stott, John R. W. *Romans: God's Good News for the World*. Downers Grove, IL: InterVarsity Press, 1994.

Stowers, Stanley K. "Apostrophe, Προσωποποιία and Paul's Rhetorical Education." Pages 351–69 in *Early Christianity and Classical Culture: Comparative Studies in Honor of Abraham J. Malherbe*. Edited by John Fitzgerald, Thomas Olbricht, and L. Michael White. NovTSup 110. Leiden: Brill, 2003.

———. *A Rereading of Romans: Justice, Jews, and Gentiles*. New Haven: Yale University Press, 1994.

Stuhlmacher, Peter. *Paul's Letter to the Romans: A Commentary*. Translated by S. J. Hafemann. Louisville: Westminster John Knox, 1994.

Thielman, Frank. *Romans*. ZECNT. Grand Rapids: Zondervan, 2018.

Timmins, Will N. *Romans 7 and Christian Identity: A Study of the "I" in Its Literary Context*. SNTSMS 170. Cambridge: Cambridge University Press, 2017.

———. "Romans 7 and the Resurrection of Lament in Christ: The Wretched 'I' and His Biblical Doppelgänger," *NovT* 61 (2019): 386–408.

———. "What's Really Going On in Romans 7." https://www. thegospelcoalition.org/article/romans-7-apostle-paul-confession/.

Vergote, Antoon. "Vie, loi et clivage du Moi dans l'épître aux Romains 7." Pages 109–47 in *Exégèse et Herméneutique*. Edited by Roland Barthes and Paul Beauchamps. Paris: Seuil, 1971.

Wasserman, Emma. "The Death of the Soul in Romans 7: Revisiting Paul's Anthropology in Light of Hellenistic Moral Psychology." *JBL* 126 (2007): 793–816.

Watkins, Edward R., Eugene Mullan, Janet Wingrove, Katharine Rimes, Herbert Steiner, Neil Bathurst, Rachel Eastman, and Jan Scott. "Rumination-Focused Cognitive-Behavioural Therapy for Residual Depression: Phase II Randomised Controlled Trial." *British Journal of Psychiatry* 199 (2011): 317–22.

Wedderburn, A. J. M. "Adam in Paul's Letter to the Romans." Pages 413–30 in *Studia Biblica 1978, 3: Papers on Paul and Other New Testament Authors*. Edited by E. A. Livingstone. JSNTSup 3. Sheffield: JSOT Press, 1980.

Wells, Kyle. *Grace and Agency in Paul and Second Temple Judaism: Interpreting the Transformation of the Heart*. NovTSup 157. Leiden: Brill, 2015.

Westerholm, Stephen. *Perspectives Old and New on Paul: The Lutheran Paul and His Critics*. Grand Rapids: Eerdmans, 2004.

Williams, Jarvis J. *One New Man: The Cross and Racial Reconciliation in Pauline Theology*. Nashville: B&H Academic, 2010.

Williams, Mark, John Teasdal, Zindel Segal, and Jon Kabat-Zinn. *The Mindful Way through Depression: Freeing Yourself from Chronic Unhappiness*. New York: Guilford, 2007.

Winger, Michael. *By What Law? The Meaning of* Nomos *in the Letters of Paul*. SBLDS 128. Atlanta: Scholars Press, 1992.

Witherington, Ben, III. *Paul's Letter to the Romans: A Socio-Rhetorical Commentary*. Grand Rapids: Eerdmans, 2004.

———. *A Socio-Rhetorical Commentary on Titus, 1–2 Timothy and 1–3 John*. Downers Grove, IL: InterVarsity Press, 2006.

Witherington, Ben, III, and Jason A. Myers. *Voices and Views on Paul: Exploring Scholarly Trends*. Downers Grove, IL: IVP Academic, 2020.

Wrede, William. *Paul*. London: Green, 1907.

Wright, N. T. "The Letter to the Romans." *NIB* 10:393–770.

———. *Paul and the Faithfulness of God*. 2 vols. Minneapolis: Fortress, 2013.

Wu, Jackson. *Reading Romans with Eastern Eyes: Honor and Shame in Paul's Message and Mission*. Downers Grove, IL: IVP Academic, 2019.

Ziesler, John A. "The Role of the Tenth Commandment in Romans 7." *JSNT* 10.33 (1988): 41–56.

Subject and Author Index

M

Scripture and Other Ancient Witnesses Index

Early Christian Writings

Greco–Roman Literature

ALSO AVAILABLE
FROM LEXHAM PRESS

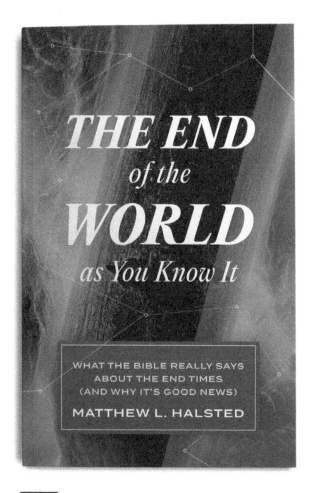

Visit lexhampress.com to learn more